A YELLOW RAFT
IN BLUE WATER

Michael Dorris

TECHNICAL DIRECTOR Maxwell Krohn
EDITORIAL DIRECTOR Justin Kestler
MANAGING EDITOR Ben Florman

SERIES EDITORS Boomie Aglietti, Justin Kestler
PRODUCTION Christian Lorentzen, Camille Murphy

WRITER James Patrick Duffy
EDITORS Matt Blanchard, Boomie Aglietti, Thomas Connors

This edition published by Spark Publishing

Spark Publishing
A Division of SparkNotes LLC
120 Fifth Avenue, 8th Floor
New York, NY 10011

02 03 04 05 SN 9 8 7 6 5 4 3 2 1

Please send all comments and questions or report errors to
feedback@sparknotes.com.

Library of Congress information available upon request

Printed and bound in the United States

RRD-C

ISBN 1-58663-495-X

INTRODUCTION: STOPPING TO BUY SPARKNOTES ON A SNOWY EVENING

Whose words these are you *think* you know.
Your paper's due tomorrow, though;
We're glad to see you stopping here
To get some help before you go.

Lost your course? You'll find it here.
Face tests and essays without fear.
Between the words, good grades at stake:
Get great results throughout the year.

Once school bells caused your heart to quake
As teachers circled each mistake.
Use SparkNotes and no longer weep,
Ace every single test you take.

Yes, books are lovely, dark, and deep,
But only what you grasp you keep,
With hours to go before you sleep,
With hours to go before you sleep.

Contents

CONTEXT

MICHAEL DORRIS WAS BORN in Louisville, Kentucky, in 1945. His heritage was mixed, as he was descended from European ancestry and from the Native American Modoc Tribe of California. Dorris spent his childhood in Kentucky but made frequent visits to reservations in the Pacific Northwest.

Later in life Dorris noted that, as a child, he never encountered Native American literary characters with whom he could identify. So after graduating cum laude from Georgetown University and earning a master's degree at Yale University, Dorris began writing, hoping to create such characters himself. He was a prolific author, publishing fourteen books and over one hundred articles between 1977 and his death in 1997. *A Yellow Raft in Blue Water*, published in 1987, was Dorris's first novel. During his writing career, Dorris remained heavily involved in academia, starting the Native American Studies program at Dartmouth College, where he taught intermittently for twenty-five years. At Dartmouth, Dorris also met his future wife and literary partner, the novelist Louise Erdrich. She too is of Native American descent, a member of the Turtle Mountain Chippewa Tribe of the Midwest.

Dorris and Erdrich had three children together, who joined the three children whom Dorris had adopted prior to his marriage. Dorris's adopted children, who were born on Native American reservations, all suffered from fetal alcohol syndrome, a variable group of birth defects that can occur in the children of women who consume large quantities of alcohol during pregnancy. One of Dorris's best-known works, *The Broken Cord* (1989), is based on the troubles and triumphs he experienced in dealing with fetal alcohol syndrome in the older of his two adopted sons, Abel.

Although the press frequently idealized Dorris's relationship with Erdrich as a literary marriage of the highest sort, the two gradually grew apart and separated. The rest of Dorris's personal life began to splinter as well: in 1991 Abel was killed in a hit-and-run accident, and in 1994 another of his adopted children, Jeffrey, accused both Dorris and Erdrich of abuse and brought a lawsuit against them. Dorris and Erdrich also began to bump heads over custody of their natural children. With his personal life already under considerable scrutiny, Dorris faced increased pressure as accusations that he had sexually abused a child leaked to the press in December of 1996. Formal charges were never brought against Dorris, but he began to suffer from severe depression from the thought that they might be. Apparently fearful of the prospect of a feeding frenzy by law enforcement officials and the media, Dorris killed himself in a motel room in Concord, New Hampshire, on April 10, 1997.

Although his tumultuous personal life and tragically short career have at times threatened to overshadow his literary accomplishments, critics acknowledge Dorris as a highly original voice in modern Native American literature, the peer of other prominent writers such as N. Scott Momaday, Sherman Alexie, and Leslie Marmon Silko.

Plot Overview

THE NOVEL IS DIVIDED INTO three sections narrated by three different Native American women: Rayona, Christine, and Ida. Rayona's narrative begins at the hospital, where she is playing cards with her mother, Christine, who drinks heavily and is frequently hospitalized. Rayona's father, Elgin, arrives and argues with Christine. Rayona leaves for the parking lot and finds Christine trying to break into their car. Christine says she is going to crash the car so Rayona can collect the life insurance payment. Rayona forces her way into the car and she and her mother drive off. Christine decides to leave their home in Seattle and return to the reservation in Montana where she grew up. Christine and Rayona spend the night packing and leave the next day.

The car breaks down a mile away from Christine's mother's house, and Christine and Rayona walk the rest of the way. Christine's mother, Ida (whom they both call Aunt Ida), is not glad to see Christine. Christine runs off, leaving Rayona with Ida. Rayona does not enjoy the reservation. Aunt Ida is cold and distant, and the other children make fun of Rayona's dark skin. The only place Rayona finds attention is at the local mission, where a priest named Father Tom persuades her to join the God Squad, a religious youth group.

Father Tom invites Rayona to a religious jamboree. They arrive early, so they stop for a while at nearby Bearpaw Lake. The two go swimming, and Father Tom suddenly makes suggestive advances toward Rayona. Embarrassed, he decides they should just return to the reservation. Rayona wants to go back to Seattle, so Father Tom arranges a train ticket for her. Rayona intentionally misses the train and sleeps by the tracks. The next day Rayona meets a gas station attendant named Sky, whose wife, Evelyn, sets Rayona up with a custodial job at Bearpaw Lake State Park. Rayona stays with Sky and Evelyn for the whole summer and makes up a family history, telling Sky and Evelyn that her parents are away for the summer. When Evelyn discovers Rayona is lying, Rayona confesses her real story.

Evelyn wants to take Rayona back to the reservation, but Rayona is confident that they will find her mother at a nearby rodeo. Rayona runs into Foxy Cree, one of the kids from the reservation.

Foxy is supposed to ride in the rodeo but is too drunk to do so, so he convinces Rayona to ride in his place. Rayona performs valiantly in the rodeo and wins a prize for her persistence. Dayton, who owns the horse that Rayona rides and who is also Christine's on-and-off boyfriend, takes Rayona back to his house. Christine is there, and she and Rayona immediately get in a fight. The next morning Christine and Rayona have a conversation out in the yard. Christine tells the story of how she had lost her faith when the world had not ended on New Year's Day of 1960 as her religious teacher had predicted it would.

The narrative voice switches to Christine, whose story begins soon after the night when the predicted end of the world did not occur. As kids, Christine and her brother, Lee, are constant companions. Christine is very daring until she loses her nerve one day while trying to cross a natural bridge on a dare. A boy named Dayton moves to the reservation and begins following Lee everywhere. Christine decides she likes Dayton, and, thinking he is interested in her, tries to seduce him. Dayton rejects Christine, however, saying he thinks of her as a sister.

After high school, Christine works for the tribal council and goes out with many boys. She has a fight with Ida and goes to live with Ida's sister, Pauline. When the Vietnam War begins, Lee tells Christine that he plans to dodge the draft but Christine tries to persuade him otherwise. She knows that if Lee dodges the draft it will hurt both her reputation and his prospects for a political career as a leader of the reservation. Dayton sees Christine's point and persuades Lee to enlist.

Christine leaves the reservation for Seattle, where she goes through many jobs and apartments. One day she receives a letter from Dayton saying that Lee is missing in action. That night she meets an army corporal named Elgin in a bar and they begin a relationship. Christine eventually realizes she is pregnant. She tells Elgin and he proposes to her. Christine and Elgin grow apart after their wedding. Just before her baby is born, Christine receives a letter from Dayton saying that Lee is dead. Christine names her baby girl Rayona and leaves Elgin when Rayona is nine months old. The two get back together occasionally, but it never lasts long.

The army finally returns Lee's body to the reservation, and Christine takes Rayona to the funeral. Christine discovers that everyone on the reservation blames her for Lee's death because she had encouraged him to enlist. Christine returns to Seattle and tries to do a good job of raising Rayona. Ida stays with them for a week while she is in town to visit her aunt Clara in the hospital, but returns to the reservation.

Christine's doctor tells her that her liver and pancreas are near failure and that she only has about six months left to live. She does not know how to react and tries to pretend everything is normal when Rayona comes to visit her. Christine tries to reconcile with Elgin, but he leaves the hospital abruptly. Christine decides her only option is to crash her car so Rayona can collect the insurance money. She tries to break into the car but Rayona catches her and they drive off together. Christine again plans to kill herself by crashing but is thwarted when the car runs out of gas. Christine then decides to return to the reservation so that Ida can look after Rayona when Christine dies.

Ida is not glad to see Christine, so Christine runs off. Foxy picks Christine up on the roadside and drives her to Dayton's house. Christine's arrival surprises Dayton, but he takes her in. The two settle into a comfortable routine, but Christine grows sicker. One day Ida comes over and says that Rayona has gone missing. Foxy and Dayton go to a rodeo with one of Dayton's horses. Dayton returns with Rayona, who promptly gets in a fight with Christine. The next morning, however, Christine and Rayona seem to have reconciled somewhat, and Christine teaches Rayona to drive. Several weeks later, the two take a road trip and have lunch together at a diner.

The narrative voice switches to Ida. When Ida is a girl, her mother becomes sick, and her aunt Clara comes to help around the house. Ida likes Clara from the start, but her father, Lecon, acts strangely around Clara. One night, Ida comes home to find both her mother and Clara crying. She learns that Clara is pregnant and that Lecon is the father. Lecon is worried about the shame this pregnancy will bring on his family, so Clara suggests that the family claim that the child is Ida's. They consult with Father Hurlburt, a trusted priest from the local mission, who suggests a motherhouse in Colorado where Clara can go to have her baby.

The nuns at the motherhouse in Colorado name Clara's baby Christine. Clara wants to give Christine up for adoption, but Ida refuses and takes Christine back to Montana while Clara stays in Colorado. Ida raises Christine until Clara returns several years later and says she has lined up a family to adopt Christine. Ida wants to keep Christine, so she has Father Hurlburt bring over the documents that say Ida is Christine's legal mother. Clara is furious and leaves.

Ida's mother dies, her father runs off, and her sister, Pauline, gets married. Willard Pretty Dog, a boy from the reservation whom Ida had a crush on in high school, returns from World War II badly disfigured by a land mine. Ida and Willard end up in a relationship and live together. While Willard is in the hospital for reconstructive surgery, Ida realizes she is pregnant. When Willard's operation successfully restores his good looks, his mother tells him to dump Ida because he can now have any girl he wants. Willard replies that even though Ida is neither pretty nor smart, she is loyal, and for that reason he wants to stay with her. But after Ida hears Willard's assessment of her, she no longer wants to live with him and he goes home.

Ida's son, Lee, is born and is a fussy child. One day Lee comes home bragging that he had to save his sister, Christine, because she got scared trying to cross a natural bridge. From that point, Lee becomes more confident as he grows older, while Christine turns inward and becomes devoutly religious. Christine suddenly begins to fear that she is going to hell. Ida consults Father Hurlburt, who says Christine's fears likely stem from a religious prophecy that has caught on among some of the kids in Christine's school. The prophecy claims that the world will end on New Year's Day of 1960, when the pope is to open a letter supposedly written by the Virgin Mary. Ida humors Christine and follows all of her instructions in preparing for the apocalypse. When New Year's Eve comes without any signs that the world is ending, Lee mocks both Christine and Ida, and Christine goes to bed very upset. Early on New Year's morning, Father Hurlburt stops by Ida's house. The two go up to sit on the roof, and in the darkness Ida begins to braid her hair.

CHARACTER LIST

Rayona A half-black, half-Native American teenager, the daughter of Christine and Elgin. Rayona is unusually tall and thin, and is very self-conscious about her physical appearance. A very intelligent girl, Rayona is also remarkably observant, though sometimes her ignorance of the world leaves her at a disadvantage. She loves her parents but is repeatedly disappointed by them, and she often feels unloved and unwanted. She dreams about having a perfect family, and invents one based on a letter she finds on the ground while working as a custodian at Bearpaw Lake. Eventually, Rayona becomes satisfied with her real family and abandons her fantasy of an ideal family.

Christine Clara and Lecon's daughter. Christine is raised as Ida's daughter, although she is actually Ida's half-sister and cousin. Christine is fickle in her youth, going from fearless to devoutly religious, but she loses her faith after an apocalyptic prophecy fails to come true. After her disillusionment with religion, Christine devotes her time to being popular and chasing boys. Christine is very protective of her brother, Lee, and always concerned for his welfare. She is self-sufficient, but is also hopelessly devoted to Elgin, Rayona's father. Christine tries to be a better mother to Rayona than Ida was to her but nonetheless engages in excessive partying and drinking that irreparably damage her liver and pancreas.

Ida Lecon's daughter. Although she poses as Christine's mother, Ida is actually Christine's half-sister and cousin: they share a father, and Christine's mother is the sister of Ida's mother. Ida is often bitter and attempts to distance herself from others, as she fears

7

becoming too attached to or dependent upon anyone. Ida feels she has spent her entire life being taken by the flow of things. She stands firm only to maintain custody of Christine.

Lecon   Ida's father, who has an affair with Clara that results in the birth of Christine. Lecon runs off shortly after Ida's mother dies, and does not return.

Clara   Ida's aunt on her mother's side, who has an affair with her brother-in-law, Lecon. Clara is Christine's biological mother, but the family hides this fact to avoid disgrace. Ida assumes control of Christine's upbringing during the time Clara lives in Denver. When Clara returns to the reservation and attempts to take Christine away, Ida asserts her legal rights to the girl, and Clara leaves bitterly.

Dayton Nickles Lee's best friend in high school, who shared the entire reservation's high hopes for Lee. Dayton and Christine would often fight for Lee's affections, and Dayton thinks of Christine as a sister. After Lee's death, Dayton shares a connection with Christine because of their relationship with Lee.

Lee   Ida's son with Willard Pretty Dog, Lee grows up thinking he is Christine's brother. Initially a timid boy, Lee becomes the most attractive young man on the reservation. Sometimes mocking in his pride, he is sure that he will have the great future that the entire reservation imagines for him.

Elgin Taylor Christine's husband and Rayona's father. Elgin has good intentions but never follows through. He seems to care for Christine, but never stays with her for long; he claims to want to be there for Rayona, but never is. He and Christine have an on-and-off relationship that typically runs hot for a few weeks and cold for much longer periods.

Father Hurlburt A priest on the mission who first becomes acquainted with Ida's family after the affair between Clara and Lecon. Father Hurlburt has a unique connection with Ida because, after the death of her parents, he is the only person on the reservation who knows the truth of Christine's lineage. Ida and Father Hurlburt share a special, though often unarticulated, friendship. He is one of the few people who seems to understand Ida, and he is always there when she needs him.

Father Tom Novak A new cleric at the Holy Martyrs Mission who recruits Rayona into the God Squad. Father Tom is the only person on the reservation who seems to think Rayona is worth his time. The two spend a lot of time together, if only because Rayona has no one else to whom she can relate. However, their close friendship ends awkwardly when Father Tom's friendship turns to lechery at Bearpaw Lake.

Willard Pretty Dog The most attractive boy on the reservation when Ida is young. Willard comes back from World War II horribly scarred. After some matchmaking by Father Hurlburt, Willard takes up with Ida and fathers Lee. After his looks are restored through reconstructive surgery, Willard is willing to stay with Ida out of duty, but when Ida realizes his take on their relationship, she sends him home.

Sky The owner of a gas station near Bearpaw Lake. Sky is kind and giving, but also rather simpleminded. He takes things as they come, and Rayona appreciates his good humor.

Evelyn Sky's wife and a cook at Bearpaw Lake State Park. Evelyn is strong willed, understanding, and caring. She likes Rayona and tries to look out for her.

Pauline   Ida's sister. Pauline leaves their parents while Ida and Clara are away in Colorado and goes to work with the nuns at the Holy Martyrs Mission. Although Pauline cares about Ida and her family, she is often disapproving. Pauline's strong religious faith and identity sometimes make her unbearably confident and self-righteous.

Foxy   Pauline and Dale Cree's son. Foxy, whose real name is Kennedy, is a cruel boy. He taunts and even threatens Rayona, and always makes her very uncomfortable.

Analysis of Major Characters

Rayona

Rayona is the product of generations of struggle and misunderstanding, and her coming-of-age is made especially difficult by the problems that have plagued her family since Ida first agreed to pose as Christine's mother. Much of Rayona's past is kept from her by her mother, Christine, and by Ida. However, Rayona is not aware of this secrecy so she does not know to look behind it or to seek to understand why her mother and presumed grandmother behave so strangely toward her. For this reason, she takes their actions at face value, often grossly misunderstanding them. Most of the time, Rayona's innate alertness and capacity for acute observation cause her to draw conclusions about people based solely on their actions and without taking their situations into account. To some extent, the novel can be seen as an argument against this highly literal way of perceiving the world.

Rayona is constantly trying to find her place and identity in the world, a task made especially difficult by her lack of information regarding her heritage. Since she has so little sense of self, Rayona often forms opinions of herself based on the way she thinks others see her: "[t]oo big, too smart, not Black, not Indian, not friendly." Rayona longs to be normal, to fit in, and especially to find a less dysfunctional family life. The family Rayona sees described in the letter she finds at Bearpaw Lake becomes her ideal. Rayona feels that a family should be the one place where she is always welcome, and it takes her most of the novel to realize that hers is one of those families after all.

Despite Rayona's disappointments and frustrations, her story ends on an optimistic note and she emerges as the future of her family. When Ida begins her story, she explains that she may one day tell it to Rayona, "who might understand." Rayona is therefore one of the few characters in the novel who may have the opportunity both to understand her past and to take control of her future. If any character in the novel can finally break from the bonds of secrecy, shame, guilt, and misunderstanding, it is Rayona.

CHRISTINE

Christine is remarkable for the dramatic differences between her inner self and the self she presents to those around her. In the eyes of her daughter, Rayona, Christine appears to be irrational and irresponsible—hardly the attributes of an ideal mother. But when Christine has the opportunity to tell her story, her behavior becomes more understandable. Christine's main problem in relationships with others, especially with Rayona, is her inability to translate her feelings into actions. This weakness naturally causes problems between Christine and Rayona, as Rayona tends to judge others based solely upon their actions.

Christine passes through a number of different stages and personalities in her life. She is first bold and brave, then deeply religious, and finally reckless. This irresponsibility continues even after Rayona is born: Christine takes her child to bars when she cannot find a babysitter. Because Christine does not makes a transition from being the life of the party to being a mother, she cannot fulfill the role that Rayona imagines a mother should. It is not until she knows she is dying that Christine really begins to act like a mother, after she realizes that Rayona will be all that is left of her life once she is gone.

Christine is the bridge between old and new in the novel. She is responsible for Rayona's knowledge of the world, but her own misunderstandings are compounded as they are passed on to her daughter. She is connected both to the city and to the reservation, and both places shape her personality. She represents a transition from old to new, during the difficult period when old problems have yet to fully heal but new ones are already beginning.

IDA

Ida is by far the most mysterious and taciturn character in the novel. Christine and Rayona know the world Ida has created for them but almost nothing of the family before her. Ida's entire relationship with the world is built on lies from the time she is fifteen years old (the same age Rayona is in her section of the novel). Manipulated and betrayed by people she trusted, Ida commits herself to withdrawing from the world and refuses to interact except on her own terms. Her silence creates confusion and misunderstanding in the lives of the children she raises, and this confusion and misunderstanding are in turn passed on to Rayona. After Ida's parents and aunt uproot her life, Ida does her best to lay a new foundation, but what she builds is shaky enough to make the lives of the future generations unsteady.

Unlike Christine, Ida does not grow and change. As she herself puts it, "I never grew up, but I got old." Ida is an old woman, but her emotions have never grown or evolved. Ida goes to the motherhouse in Colorado with Clara and returns with a baby, but otherwise she is unchanged. Ida spends every day in the same routine of chores. She improves her house and adds television to her schedule, but for the most part does the same thing every day. The only man she ever pursues is Willard, her old childhood crush. Much of this paralysis comes from Ida's determination not to become emotionally attached to anyone, and her desire to remain safely within her sphere of control prevents her from ever trying new things.

Ida represents the secret heritage of her family, and the wounds we see Rayona coping within the "Rayona" section of the novel had in fact been inflicted in Ida's time. Thus, although Ida speaks her part in the last section of the novel, she also represents the beginning of the story, and it is to her that we must turn to understand fully the stories that Christine and Rayona have to tell.

CHARACTER ANALYSIS

THEMES, MOTIFS & SYMBOLS

THEMES

Themes are the fundamental and often universal ideas explored in a literary work.

UNDERSTANDING DIFFERENT PERSPECTIVES

Misunderstandings between characters occur throughout the novel, and Dorris puts us in the unusual position of being able to see both sides of some arguments. There are three different but overlapping story lines with three different narrators who occasionally report the same event from differing points of view. These multiple narrators demonstrate how three characters who should be very close to one another can misunderstand each other, at times dramatically. As the novel opens, for example, Rayona is at the hospital visiting Christine, whose actions seem melodramatic, irresponsible, and irrational. However, when this scene is revisited in Christine's story, we learn that Christine has just found out she has less than six months to live, and she wounded by the lack of sympathy from both her daughter and her ex-husband.

Likewise, though Ida comes off as rather cold and resentful to others—she herself admits this is an apt description—her personal life at least makes her temperament seem forgivable or understandable. If Christine and Rayona knew Ida's history, they would understand that her coldness is her reaction to the treatment she has received throughout her life. Dorris presents the defining events of his characters' lives, the ones that shape who they are and how they react to the world. In the cases of Christine and Ida, such events often remain secret and inspire negative reactions from the novel's other characters. Only when we are given access to a character's life and thoughts can we hope to understand that character's actions.

THE EFFECT OF EVENTS ON LATER GENERATIONS

In the end, *A Yellow Raft in Blue Water* favors family as a means of support, but the novel also questions how the problems of one generation can be passed to the next. Ida, Christine, and Rayona each represent a different generation of the same family, and each generation resonates with the lives of those who came before. The secrets that characterize Ida's life create a number of misunderstandings between the three women. Neither Rayona nor Christine can understand the events that influence them, and a great deal of confusion and misunderstanding grows between mother and daughter. The events surrounding Christine's birth and adoption by Ida resonate throughout the novel. Ida is the only person to witness these events, but they are so powerful that they affect the way she raises Christine, who in turn passes their effect on to Rayona.

FINDING A TRUE IDENTITY

Finding one's place is a crucial element of growing up, and since growing up is a part of each of the novel's three stories, each of the three chief characters struggles to belong. Ida never really has the opportunity to find her place or assert herself, and she quickly gives up any hope of successfully battling the currents that drive her life. Ida tries to come to peace with the path her life has taken but she remains resentful. Christine, on the other hand, has many opportunities that Ida lacks, and she takes full advantage of them. Christine tries on a number of identities, looking for one that fits: she tries first to be daring, then religious, then social and even somewhat promiscuous. None of these identities fulfills Christine, however, so she looks for herself in other people. She finds comfort in being Lee's sister, and then Elgin's husband, but the comfort does not last. Only when Rayona is born does Christine find her true place. She feels that Rayona gives her life meaning, and though she continues to live her wild life, she knows that, in the end, whatever she does must be for Rayona.

Rayona's identity is more precarious than her mother's. Although Rayona knows the identities of her parents, Elgin is largely absent and Christine is not exactly motherly. Rayona longs for a place in a family, so she clings to the love expressed in the letter she finds at Bearpaw Lake instead of looking to something that is actually part of her life. Rayona also struggles with her racial and physical identity, as she is of mixed race and gangly appearance. She is an outsider in almost every way and indulges in escapism. Once Rayona discards Ellen's letter, however, we see that she finally comes to feel comfortable with her mother and her own identity. For Rayona, an integral part of finding her identity is trying on a fictitious one and realizing that even the dreamiest circumstances she can imagine do not make her hurt less. Rayona's journey is ultimately less about figuring out who she is than it is about reconciling herself to her identity.

MOTIFS

Motifs are recurring structures, contrasts, or literary devices that can help to develop and inform the text's major themes.

POP CULTURE

References to popular culture appear consistently throughout the novel and help to color the eras and places that the three protagonists describe. Ida, Christine, and Rayona all listen to music and talk about the songs they hear. Christine invests significance in her two rented videos, Ida watches soap operas every day, and Rayona refers to brands of soft drinks. Ida, Christine, and Rayona are all products of the time period in which they grow up, and having a real grasp of when and where they live helps us understand the characters themselves. Lee's death, for instance, a traumatic event for both Ida and Christine, would never have occurred if not for the Vietnam War. These references to popular culture thus help situate the story and characters, which is especially important in a novel that presents forty-two years of time in a non-linear fashion.

FAITH

Faith is one of the more elusive elements of the novel, but it is an issue that each of the protagonists confronts. Rayona, Christine, and Ida have very different experiences with faith and the church. Rayona, abandoned by her parents and ignored by Ida, turns to the church for security. In her relationship with Father Tom, it appears as if Rayona has found someone who cares about her and whom she can trust. However, the basis for this trust turns out to be illusory, and in the end Rayona finds the security she needs only with her mother. Ida, on the other hand, does find a meaningful relationship, and the closest thing she has to a mutual understanding, in her relationship with Father Hurlburt. In contrast to the somewhat devious Father Tom, Father Hurlburt is one of the few people who shares Ida's secrets. At times Father Hurlburt seems to be the only person who thinks Ida is worth being around. Ida has not lived a perfect life by Christian standards, something that her sister, Pauline, is sure to point out. Father Hurlburt, however, never judges Ida, and he is able to look past religious dogma and become her close friend. Finally, Christine's religious faith wavers over the course of her life. She shows a strong capacity for faith in her early life, but when a critical element of her faith is proven wrong, Christine completely turns her back on religion.

Most of the religious figures in the novel are portrayed as malicious, absurd, or a combination of both. Though resentment toward the presence of the Holy Martyrs Mission on the reservation is obvious from the very beginning of the novel, a feeling lingers that faith is good and helpful for whomever it touches. For Rayona, Ida, and Christine, faith is sometimes vague or obscured, even warped and dangerous, yet it can support them when they least expect it.

SYMBOLS

Symbols are objects, characters, figures, or colors used to represent abstract ideas or concepts.

VIDEOS

When Christine rents Christine and Little Big Man at Village Video, she describes the movies as Rayona's inheritance, but they come to stand as more than just physical gifts. Christine chooses the videos specifically because they are films that show the kind of tough determination that Christine hopes Rayona sees in her. When Christine is gone, the movies remind Rayona of her and become surrogates for her physical presence. When Christine, Rayona, Ida, and Dayton watch the films together, they create a final memory of unity and come to stand for family harmony as well. Christine picks the movies with ambitious goals, yet they exceed even her expectations and shape the legacy they are supposed to symbolize.

ELLEN'S LETTER

Rayona finds a torn letter on the ground while she is doing custodial work at Bearpaw Lake State Park. The letter becomes Rayona's symbol of the perfect family. In fact, the piece of paper Rayona finds is just a fragment that does not say too much, but the basic ideas it includes—having parents on good enough terms that they will sign a letter together—are so foreign to Rayona that she magnifies them into the rosiest portrait imaginable. Only when Rayona has breakfast with her mother at a diner several weeks later does she throw the letter away, a gesture that indicates that Rayona has finally found peace with her real family.

BRAIDS

References to braids are made subtly throughout *A Yellow Raft In Blue Water*, and they become a symbol of how the lives of different family members, like the different parts of the story, can overlap and form a more complete whole. The most prominent of these references is the one that ends the novel, when Father Hurlburt and Ida go up to her roof on the night that the world is supposed to end and she starts braiding her hair in the darkness. Dorris ends the novel with this image because it is an apt symbol for the novel itself. The stories told by Rayona, Christine, and Ida are all part of a greater story, and this story can be told in full only if their narratives are looked at together. Therefore, Dorris uses the image of the braid—three strands of hair that are woven together, pulled one over the other and merged—to illustrate further how his novel and the lives of its characters overlap and complement each other.

Summary & Analysis

Chapter 1

Summary: Chapter 1

The first of three sections in *A Yellow Raft in Blue Water* is titled "Rayona," and Rayona narrates it. As the story begins, Rayona is sitting in the Indian Health Service (IHS) hospital in Seattle with her Native American mother, Christine. The two are playing cards, and Christine wins a hand just as Rayona's father, a black man named Elgin, appears. Christine tries to shoo Rayona away, but Elgin asks Rayona to stay, wanting to have a look at her. Rayona, who is very tall and skinny, suddenly feels self-conscious about her appearance.

Elgin has come to the hospital to drop off Christine's car, a Volaré, but Christine insists that Elgin use the car to pick her up when she leaves the hospital. Elgin protests, saying that Christine really does not look that sick. Secretly, Rayona shares Elgin's views on Christine's health. Christine becomes quite angry when she hears Elgin claim she is not as sick as she thinks. As Elgin tries to shoo Rayona from the room, Christine tells him to go back to his "little black girl." Elgin goes, leaving the keys to the Volaré with Rayona, who also makes a hasty exit.

Rayona starts to think about her mother's history at the hospital. Christine visits the hospital frequently, always after long nights of partying and drinking. When Christine gets home, however, she is ready to start partying again and the cycle repeats. Her best friend, Charlene, frequently cautions her that her body cannot take so much punishment, but she always shrugs off such warnings.

As Rayona wanders the hospital, her thoughts drift back to her father and she wonders where he might be. Her mother has always claimed that she and Elgin separated because of their racial difference, but Rayona has heard this too many times to believe it. Rayona has tried every trick she knows to get her father to notice her, but they almost never see each other.

Rayona goes to the parking lot to find the Volaré, but when she reaches it, a hospital worker is trying to open the door with a coat hanger. Rayona accosts the worker, only to discover that it is her mother dressed in nurse's clothes stolen from the hospital. Christine, feeling oppressed by her troubles, says that she has decided to crash the car so that Rayona can benefit from the insurance payments.

Rayona explains that Christine frequently makes similar threats, saying she plans to go to the place where Elgin proposed to her to kill herself. However, she never does. Skeptical, Rayona forces her way into the car, and they drive off. When they near their destination, Christine pulls over and tells Rayona to get out. Rayona dares her mother to go, but the car stalls when Christine tries to start it. The car is out of gas. After a short argument, Rayona and Christine set out for a gas station a few miles down the road. By the time they get there, Christine is in a good mood again.

ANALYSIS: CHAPTER I

From Rayona's point of view, Christine is acting irrationally and absurdly in this chapter. Her actions seem to be all an act, a show put on to gain Rayona's and Elgin's sympathy. However, neither is willing to give Christine what she wants, and from the information that Dorris shares with us in this first chapter we do not find it difficult to share Rayona's skepticism regarding her mother's illness. Dorris tells us, for example, that Christine's partying frequently puts her in the hospital but that she is too irresponsible to calm down. Dorris also shows us that even though Christine accuses Elgin of having left her for a black girl, she has made this accusation so many times that it is not credible. Finally, when Christine appears in the parking lot, she is wearing clothing that makes her unrecognizable to her own daughter, as if her very personality were camouflaged and hidden. Although Rayona never expressly tells us not to trust Christine, Rayona's confusion and mistrust of her mother are evident in the facts she chooses to relate and the skeptical way in which she tells them.

From the very beginning of the chapter, Rayona is isolated from both her mother and father, and strong familial ties are missing. Her irritation with her mother prevents Rayona from taking her mother seriously and from enjoying their time together. Elgin appears rather disinterested in both Rayona and Christine. Unlike Christine, Rayona does not react to Elgin's indifference overtly. However, as Rayona articulates her inner thoughts to us, it is easy to tell how hurt she is, not only by Elgin's show of apathy at the IHS but also by the course of her life in general.

Rayona's odd appearance compounds her outsider status and awkwardness with her parents. Nearly everyone notices Rayona's lankiness: even her father focuses his gaze on her size and weight when he enters the hospital. Rayona is so accustomed to comments about her frame that she is acutely sensitive to any comments she receives that are about some other aspect of her. In addition to her physical awkwardness, Rayona is somewhat self-conscious of her skin color. With a black father and Native American mother, Rayona feels like an outsider to both races, and the color of her skin makes her outsider status impossible to hide. We see Rayona's racial self-consciousness in the frequent comments she makes about the difference between her skin tone and that of either of her parents.

Rayona also pays particular attention to popular culture, making special note of the songs she hears on the radio and the brand of car her mother drives. Rayona also frequently works pop culture into her analogies, metaphors, and similes, which is not surprising for a girl her age. These repeated references to popular culture remind us that Rayona desperately wants to fit in.

CHAPTER 2

SUMMARY: CHAPTER 2

> I listen, eavesdropping into her life, while she lights
> Kent after Kent and the room fills with smoke while
> she kills the bottle.
>
> (See QUOTATIONS, p. 74)

Rayona and Christine put three gallons of gas into the Volaré. Christine decides that they are going to go to Aunt Ida's, and that they should leave right away. Rayona reflects on her mother's few ties to Seattle, the most notable of which is her lifetime membership to Village Video. Christine had seen an advertisement for a ninety-nine-cent membership the week before her last visit to the hospital and decided it was too good a deal to pass up, even though she does not own a VCR. When Christine and Rayona had arrived at Village Video to sign up they saw a woman arguing with the store manager because she had bought a membership just four days earlier that had cost her significantly more. Christine was delighted at the woman's loss. Christine and Rayona also learned that the special offer was for lifetime membership and Christine therefore decided that the membership should be in Rayona's name because she would retain her membership at Village Video even after Christine's death. The memory of her mother's words—"'Till death"—as Rayona signed the Village Video contract gives Rayona a strangely depressed feeling. Rayona remembers that the week after they got the membership at Village Video, Christine checked into the hospital.

Later that night, Christine and Rayona pack for the trip to Aunt Ida's. They fill four trash bags with various things and do not finish until five in the morning. Rayona wants to leave right away but Christine insists on waiting a few hours so she can stop at Village Video. They wait for the store to open, rent Christine and Little Big Man, and then set off for Montana. As she drives, Christine starts to talk about Aunt Ida, her adoptive mother whom she believes is her biological mother. Aunt Ida is actually Christine's mother, but since Ida was unmarried when Christine was born, she decided to have Christine and her son, Lee, both call her "aunt." Christine asks Rayona if she will miss anyone in Seattle, then quickly concludes that Rayona won't. Rayona knows her mother is right because they have moved around too much for Rayona to make any friends.

After a couple days of driving, Christine and Rayona arrive in Montana. Less than a mile before they reach Aunt Ida's, Christine accidentally drives the Volaré into a dip in the road, and it stalls. The car will not start up again, so they start walking. Aunt Ida is not glad to see Christine and asks her for three reasons why she should welcome Christine home. Christine gives two reasons—that she is Ida's daughter and that she needs a place to stay—but as a third reason she can only think of "go fuck yourself anyway." After she spits this third reason at Ida, Christine turns and runs back down the road. Rayona tries to follow her but cannot keep up. A passing pickup truck stops for Christine, and Rayona collapses furiously into the dirt by the side of the road. Aunt Ida comes for Rayona, and the two walk back toward the house.

ANALYSIS: CHAPTER 2

Rayona's portrayal of her mother's actions continues to be less than flattering. She finds Christine's membership to Village Video absurd since they do not own a VCR. From Rayona's point of view, Christine's enthusiasm over the membership deal at Village Video seems impractical and ridiculous. In addition, Christine's decision to put Rayona's name on the membership seems rather selfish, especially when she comes back a week later and rents two videos with no intention of returning them—Christine's own interpretation of what "lifetime membership" means.

As Christine and Rayona drive away from Seattle, Rayona's already severe sense of isolation becomes even more profound. Leaving Seattle gives Rayona the opportunity to reflect that she has never stayed anywhere long enough to have friends. She has always been the new kid, avoided because she is "[t]oo big, too smart, not Black, not Indian, not friendly." Elgin, her father, is the only person in Seattle Rayona might conceivably miss, but she has largely given up on him. The only person Rayona has is her mother, which makes Rayona's increasing disillusionment with and eventual abandonment by Christine all the more poignant. Without her mother, Rayona feels rootless and cast adrift. Infuriated and confused after Christine leaves her at the end of the chapter, Rayona has difficulty finding an appropriate outlet for her feelings. She can only tear at the ground and scream incoherently at Aunt Ida. It is not until Ida takes Rayona into her arms that Rayona is grounded again. Rayona's search for belonging has suddenly become more precarious, as she has been separated from Christine, the most stable influence in her life up to this point. All her life, her circle of family and friends has consisted almost exclusively of her mother. Left to her own devices now, Rayona must find something new to hold on to.

We continue to see popular media and culture take a prominent place in the story. Christine makes two rentals at the video store: Christine and Little Big Man. She chooses the former because of the title and the latter because she dated one of the extras. Both of these movies offer her some sort of escape from the unpleasant reality of her life. These videos follow Rayona through her subsequent adventures and become a kind of symbol for her. Pop culture also provides an important moment of foreshadowing: the song lyric Aunt Ida is singing when Rayona and Christine arrive, "Looking for love in all the wrong places," in addition to describing the emptiness that Christine finds in Ida and Rayona finds in Christine, becomes very important later in the novel when Aunt Ida and Christine get to tell their stories.

CHAPTER 3

SUMMARY & ANALYSIS

SUMMARY: CHAPTER 3

Rayona and Aunt Ida do not really know how to live with one another. Rayona lives in the room that once was her mother's, which is just the way her mother left it. Even Christine's old posters of celebrities like Elvis Presley are still up. When her own clothes get dirty, Rayona wears Christine's old ones. Rayona looks through Christine's old things, finding a notebook in which she wrote how her own first name would look paired with different boys' last names. Rayona finds a box of old pictures of Christine, including her high school graduation photo. Rayona studies the picture, trying to find resemblances between herself and her mother, but concludes that her mother looks far more saintly.

Aunt Ida watches TV on most days, primarily soap operas and The People's Court. The stupidity and ignorance of the characters in both shows infuriates her. Ida plans her work schedule around these shows and follows the same schedule every day. Ida speaks to Rayona only in her native language, which Rayona calls "Indian," but Rayona suspects that Ida also knows English.

One day an elderly man comes to visit Aunt Ida, and Rayona overhears them talking. They are discussing Rayona and her mother. Apparently Christine is living with Dayton, her old boyfriend. Seeing Rayona, the elderly man introduces himself. His name is Father Hurlburt, and he is a priest at the Holy Martyrs Mission a few miles away. Rayona is surprised the minister speaks Indian. Father Hurlburt knew Rayona when she was a baby, and comments on how she has grown so tall and thin. He asks her if she has been brought up as a Catholic, and concludes that she should join the "God Squad," a group of young people that meets at the mission regularly.

Two days later, Father Tom Novak, a talkative and enthusiastic priest who is new to the Holy Martyrs Mission, picks Rayona up for her first God Squad meeting. Two old Native Americans outside the mission mock Tom in their language, then quiet themselves as they realize that Rayona can understand them. Only two other children are inside the Mission when Rayona and Tom arrive. One is Annabelle Stiffarm, the other is Kennedy Cree, better known as Foxy. Foxy is Rayona's cousin. Foxy and Annabelle are both rather cold to Rayona, and Foxy makes a point of mentioning that Rayona's father is a "nigger." Foxy and Annabelle swiftly exit the mission. Rayona and Novak wait an hour, but no one else comes.

Rayona starts school the next week. She feels stupid in her mother's too-tight clothes and is made fun of for being half black. Rayona realizes that Tom is going to take her under his wing, as has happened so many times before. Tom is proud that he has learned some Indian from a member of the tribal council, but the council member has actually played a joke on Tom and taught him to say something obscene. Rayona is glad to have someone who seems to care about her and becomes rather friendly with Tom. In fact, she becomes the only regular member of the God Squad. Although every God Squad meeting is supposed to have a theme, Tom always ends up talking about "The Wonders of the Human Body," his euphemism for sex. Rayona does not have much knowledge on the subject, but knows that it has changed other kids her age "for the worse." When driving her home from one of the meetings, Tom asks Rayona if she has ever had any sexual dreams. Rayona doesn't know what he is talking about, but Tom says that she needs guidance, since she is growing into an "attractive young lady." He drives off, leaving Rayona somewhat baffled.

ANALYSIS: CHAPTER 3

Living in Christine's old room, Rayona is exposed to the popular culture of her mother's generation. Celebrities such as Elvis Presley, Jacqueline Kennedy, and Connie Francis firmly situate Christine's childhood in a distinct time period. This information is more than simple background, as we later learn that the culture of Christine's era profoundly shaped her life. The pop culture evident on the walls of Rayona's new room furthers her immersion into her mother's culture and upbringing. Living on the same reservation where her mother grew up is a big first step in Rayona's understanding of who Christine is, and living in a room of Elvis posters shows Rayona the other big influences in her mother's life. Nonetheless, seeing how Christine grew up does not immediately alter Rayona's opinion of her mother, and she still does not identify with Christine. When Rayona looks at her mother's graduation portrait, for example, she finds little physical resemblance between herself and the picture, which mirrors how emotionally unalike Rayona and her mother are.

Rayona frequently thinks that other people might accept her more readily if she were more pleasant to look at, which reveals how she feels physically marked as an outsider by her dark skin. Rayona thinks Annabelle and Foxy are both quite attractive, and this fact makes Rayona feels like an outsider when she is with them. On the reservation, Rayona's foreignness is jarring, as she is racially different from everyone else. When other people look at her, especially her peers, all they see is Rayona's black heritage. Even other half-Indian children crack jokes about Rayona's dark skin. Being much smarter than most of the kids in her class does not help Rayona fit in either, as the nuns at the mission school constantly single her out for praise. Ironically, although Rayona finds it hard to relate to other people her age in Seattle, she has an even harder time with the youths on the reservation and is lonelier than ever.

Rayona does find a kind of acceptance in Father Tom. In some ways, Father Tom is even more of an outsider than Rayona. He is the only person on the reservation with no Native American blood, since even Father Hurlburt is part Native American and can communicate with his parishioners. When other Indians make fun of Father Tom in a language he cannot understand, Rayona sympathizes and eventually even helps him out with the language. With no other place to belong to, Rayona finds acceptance as the only member of the God Squad. Father Tom seems to be the only person on the reservation who thinks Rayona worthwhile, so even though she sees him as somewhat foolish and ignorant, she enjoys Father Tom's company.

CHAPTER 4

SUMMARY: CHAPTER 4

Rayona decides that she wants to leave the reservation. She takes a day off from school to plan out exactly what she is going to do. Before the day is even half over, however, Father Tom shows up at Rayona's house. She tells Father Tom she is planning to leave, and though he humors her at first, Rayona quickly recognizes he will try to change her mind. She decides it will be easier if she just goes to school. Father Tom invites her to an event called the Teens for Christ Jamboree, and Rayona decides to go, if only as a way of getting off of the reservation. The day they leave, Father Tom brings Rayona by Aunt Ida's house to pack. Aunt Ida is not there, but

Rayona can tell that Christine has stopped by recently because a package that had arrived for Christine is gone, along with some things from her room. Feeling even more rejected by her mother, Rayona packs all her belongings in a plastic bag. She also takes the tapes from Village Video.

On the way to the jamboree, Father Tom asks Rayona about her family. She claims that her mother is dead and that her father is a pilot. Father Tom says that he never had a father either. Rayona points out that she does in fact have a father and asks Father Tom why he joined the priesthood. He says it was because he heard his calling to be "God's helper." Rayona falls asleep as they ride late into the night.

When Rayona wakes, they are at the same gas station where she and her mother stopped on their way to the reservation. Father Tom explains that they are a day early to the jamboree and that they will have a chance to relax. They get to a campsite at Bearpaw Lake State Park and sit down for a picnic. Father Tom cannot get the grill started, so he suggests they go for a swim instead. When they arrive at the lake, Father Tom decides the water is too cold, but Rayona sees some people swimming out beyond a yellow raft and jumps in. When she reaches the raft, Father Tom jumps in after her, but cramps up before he can reach her. Rayona jumps back into the water and saves him. After Rayona drags Father Tom onto the dock, he draws her close to him. They embrace, Father Tom "duck[s] his head," and his "hips jerk against" Rayona. Then Father Tom pulls away and says that they have experienced "an occasion of sin."

Father Tom tells Rayona that they have to go back to the reservation and that they never should have left. He says that Rayona needs to find friends her own age and that people who see the two of them together constantly might misunderstand their relationship. Rayona says she is going back to Seattle, and Tom seems to like the idea. He gives Rayona money, finds out about a train for her, and tells her that he will let Aunt Ida know where she went. That night Father Tom drives Rayona to the train and gives her his touristy bead necklace, saying they will meet again and that she will be in his prayers. After Father Tom leaves, Rayona does not get on the train and throws the necklace onto the tracks. She sits down to think and wait out the night, "happy for no reason."

ANALYSIS: CHAPTER 4

In this chapter, Rayona breaks away from her old life of ostracism, and we see her severing the ties that bind her to the reservation one by one. Rayona keeps a close eye on the package addressed to Christine, and when the package disappears, it ruins Rayona's last hope that Christine will eventually return for her. The package's disappearance becomes the final evidence for Rayona that her mother has abandoned her, and when she decides that her mother truly does not want to have anything to do with her, a vital tie to her old life is broken. Instead, on the drive to the jamboree, Rayona begins to invent a new life for herself, one in which her mother is dead and her father pilots jets. Rayona's fabrication of Christine's death is symbolic of the new detachment of daughter from mother. The fact that Rayona says Christine is dead also shows that Rayona has a very real anger toward her mother for having abandoned her.

The yellow raft in Bearpaw Lake is the raft of the novel's title, and it becomes a symbol of the time and place where Rayona breaks her final ties to her old life at the reservation. The raft becomes the launching point for Rayona's thoughts about the future, and Dorris revisits this image twice more when he relates Rayona's travels and dreams of a new life.

Rayona's encounter with Father Tom at Bearpaw Lake spoils their relationship. After the incident, Father Tom becomes nervous and appears to want to rid himself of Rayona, reversing his earlier lectures on why she should remain on the reservation. Instead of being hurt by Father Tom's eagerness to see her go, Rayona is glad, as the encounter with Father Tom has made her disillusioned with him and strengthened her resolve to go back to Seattle. Rayona does not leave for Seattle, however, and eventually decides to stay near the lake. She has broken free of virtually all association with her former life, as no one from her old life knows where she is. Now that she has gained this emotional distance from her old life, she no longer feels the need to create a physical distance from it.

Sitting by the train tracks, Rayona claims to be "happy for no reason," but the reason for her happiness is more evident to us than it is to her. Now that Rayona has severed all ties to the life she has known for fifteen years, she is free to live, or imagine the life she wants to create, and her happiness comes from this freedom. Even though her ideal life is vague and has no outline or plan, she has still escaped into a new world in which she has control of her future and can create her own life.

CHAPTER 5

SUMMARY: CHAPTER 5

This scrap of paper in my hand makes me feel poor in a way like I just heard of rich. Jealous. What kind of a person would throw it away?

(See QUOTATIONS, p. 73)

Rayona wakes the next morning and crosses the road to the entrance of Bearpaw Lake State Park. She finds a sign that instructs lost hikers to stay put. She does so, and a short time later encounters a man whom she recognizes from the gas station the day before. The man introduces himself as Sky, and Rayona follows him into the park office. He makes Rayona a cup of coffee and tells her a joke about a priest, a rabbi, and a Hindu. Rayona tells Sky that she is from Seattle, that her parents are on vacation, that her father is a pilot, and that she ran away from the priest Sky had seen her with because she didn't want to be converted. Although Rayona fabricates nearly the entire story, one element is true: that she has an uncle, Lee, who died in Vietnam.

Sky calls his wife, Evelyn, who works as a cook in the park, to see if she can get Rayona a job. Evelyn makes Rayona breakfast and sends her to see Mr. McCutcheon, the man in charge of park maintenance. Mr. McCutcheon sets Rayona up spearing trash and gives her a uniform, noting how tall and skinny Rayona is as he picks out a uniform for her. Rayona goes to the ladies' room to put on her uniform, but there is no mirror, so she goes to the men's room to check her hair. As she is leaving, Andy, Dave, and John, three college students, come into the men's room. They are also grounds workers and are envious that Rayona has been assigned to work in Zone Seven because an attractive young lifeguard works there. Rayona thinks bitterly to herself that Andy, Dave, and John treat her like one of the guys but then notes that being pretty never helped her mother very much.

There is not much trash to pick up in Zone Seven, and most of what Rayona finds has probably been there for some time. As she is about to leave, she happens upon half of a crumpled letter. The letter, addressed to some unknown camper, is from "Mother & Pops," and declares how much the parents love and miss the letter's addressee. Rayona is jealous and is going to put the letter in the trash but finds that she cannot. Instead, she deposits it in her wallet. The letter lingers in her mind and makes her miss the rains of Seattle.

ANALYSIS: CHAPTER 5

At the beginning of this chapter, Rayona has a blank slate upon which she can construct her fantasy life, and it is interesting to note which parts of her life she chooses to keep and which parts she continues to reinvent. When Rayona meets Sky, she has the opportunity to tell him anything she wants, but even as she makes up her life story, Rayona preserves several facts from her real life. One of these points of reality is Rayona's uncle, Lee. Lee died in Vietnam, and part of the reason that Rayona includes him in her narrative is because mentioning Lee helps her relate to Sky, who had dodged the draft. Rayona also chooses to keep Lee as a part of her fantasy life because he is non-threatening and never rejected her. Rayona's vague memory of Lee's funeral may be another reason why she does not turn her back on this part of her old life. Lee's funeral is Rayona's earliest conscious memory, and as such represents a beginning for Rayona. Because Lee's funeral marks the beginning of Rayona's conscious life, it is not, in her mind, as corrupted as the rest of her past, and she therefore feels it is a safe memory to hold on to. She continues, however, to deny that she has run away and to assert that her father is a pilot. Instead of saying Christine is dead, however, this time Rayona softens her view and claims that her parents are on vacation.

After her conversation with Sky, Rayona begins the first day of her new life. As she gets a job and meets a number of new people, she begins to change not just her past, but also her future. Importantly, however, Rayona learns that there are some aspects of herself that she does not have the power to rewrite. Mr. McCutcheon comments abundantly on Rayona's sex, color, height, and weight, even though he is one of the first people ever to be impressed by these attributes. Instead of rejection, Mr. McCutcheon is proud of the fact that Rayona will break new ground for the custodial department at Bearpaw Lake by being the department's first woman and first minority worker. Rayona is less pleased with the reception she receives from her fellow groundskeepers. She realizes the college boys do not really even think of her as a girl and that her unattractiveness will always limit her to being one of the boys.

The letter Rayona discovers in the dirt presents a picture of ideal family life and becomes another part of Rayona's escapist fantasy.

Reading the letter, Rayona imagines herself as its addressee. Although Rayona keeps Christine as her mother in this fantasy, she imagines Christine acting in an overtly affectionate way, something completely out of character for the real Christine. Nevertheless, the letter makes Rayona miss her mother, whom she imagines as the rains of Seattle. In earlier chapters, Rayona often describes her mother's speech as rain or water. Now, as she thinks of Christine as part of the ideal family, Rayona longs for the rains of her former hometown.

CHAPTER 6

SUMMARY: CHAPTER 6

Rayona, Sky, and Evelyn arrive at Sky and Evelyn's trailer at the end of the day. Evelyn puts on a housecoat and slippers that remind Rayona of her mother. Evelyn has bought two packs of macaroni and cheese for each of them, but Rayona falls asleep on the couch instead of having dinner. Sky and Evelyn go through Rayona's pockets while she sleeps in an attempt to find out more about her. They suspect Rayona is a runaway, but when they find the letter she picked up during her rounds, they decide she must be telling the truth. The next morning, Sky and Evelyn are groggy but Rayona is fresh and ready to start work. The three drive to work, where Evelyn makes Rayona breakfast again. Rayona can tell that Evelyn likes her, and she likes Evelyn in return.

Rayona starts her rounds. She reaches the lake where she and Father Tom went swimming and considers taking a dip, but someone is already there. Looking from behind a tree by the side of the lake, Rayona sees an attractive girl on the yellow raft. Rayona sees the girl as everything she herself is not "but ought to be." The girl is talking to someone on the shore, and Rayona overhears that her name is Ellen. Soon, Ellen dives into the water and swims away.

Rayona starts to become accustomed to her rounds. In addition to trash, she sometimes finds lost articles of clothing. Once something has been in the lost and found box for three weeks, anyone can claim it, so Rayona slowly gathers a new wardrobe for herself. Rayona sometimes also finds things for Sky and Evelyn. One day she finds a blanket that Dave, one of the college students, wants, but Rayona keeps it for Evelyn.

Rayona cannot seem to get Ellen out of her mind, so she asks around to find out what she can about the girl. Evelyn does not particularly like Ellen because "she's some kind of vegetarian," and Sky knows only that Ellen drives a red Toyota Celica and buys premium gasoline with her father's credit card. Andy's opinion of Ellen is focused mainly on her "[b]azzooms," and Dave thinks that Ellen is a "bubblehead," so Rayona gathers most of her intelligence from Ellen herself. On the morning of the Fourth of July, Ellen enters the lodge kitchen with her parents and politely asks Evelyn to make them breakfast. Ellen starts talking to Rayona, who is surprised by how much Ellen knows about her. Ellen's father shows Rayona a picture of Ellen's foster brother, a Native American child whom Ellen's parents sponsor through the Save the Children charity. The boy is named Rocky and reminds Rayona of Foxy. Ellen's father proudly explains that Rocky has begun to call him and his wife "Mother and Pops." The conversation turns to Ellen's skills with children and animals, and Ellen's mother mentions how lonely "Rascal" is now that Ellen is gone. Rayona catches Evelyn looking at her and realizes that Evelyn recognizes "Mother and Pops" and "Rascal" from the letter Rayona picked off the ground. Rayona runs from the diner and throws the letter onto the ground, but soon picks it up again, reading it and seeing her own family in her mind.

ANALYSIS: CHAPTER 6

Sky and Evelyn's house seems strangely familiar to Rayona because a number of the objects and decorations in their trailer fulfill a role similar to that of the physical details of Rayona's past. Even though Rayona never acknowledges it, the trailer is similar to Aunt Ida's house in many respects. Sky and Evelyn's trailer is full of tabloid newspapers such as the National Enquirer and the Star, the literary equivalent of the soap operas Ida watches. Evelyn's typical outfit of a sleeveless housecoat and fuzzy slippers also reminds Rayona of her past, particularly her mother. However, Rayona resists the memories and feelings that Sky and Evelyn's trailer evoke because they interfere with her attempts to make her new life as separate as possible from the one she has lived for the past fifteen years.

In Ellen, Rayona encounters the idealized embodiment of her own fabricated life. Seeing Ellen on the yellow raft, Rayona considers the girl to be everything she herself should be but is not. Rayona's quest to find out everything there is to know about Ellen is partly an attempt to become more like Ellen, at least in her fantasies. Indeed, when Rayona sees Ellen at the lake, she avoids looking for too long for fear of seeing something imperfect. Rayona maintains only limited contact with Ellen, probably out of fear of ruining her fantasy, but is able to idealize the little contact she does have.

In her interactions with Sky and Evelyn, Rayona is able to live her fantasy life to some extent, but her romanticizing is jeopardized by her encounters with Ellen. Having read the letter in Rayona's wallet, Sky and Evelyn see Rayona only in the context of the life she has made up. Because they treat Rayona like she actually lives the life described in the letter, she can imagine that she really does have two loving parents, a big house with a yard, and a dog. Rayona is free to imagine that her time at Bearpaw Lake is just a small break from her idealized real life. Rayona's fantasy breaks down, however, when she finally comes into contact with the true owner of the life she has borrowed. When Ellen and her parents come to the diner for breakfast, Evelyn recognizes in their conversation facts that she had previously attributed to Rayona. The whole purpose of Rayona's fantasy life is to make other people believe it is her reality, and when that belief evaporates, her dream world comes crashing down around her. Nonetheless, even though she is aware that her constructed life is a lie, she cannot let go of the fantasy. Rayona keeps Ellen's letter, reading it again and putting herself back into the world it creates for her.

CHAPTER 7

SUMMARY: CHAPTER 7

When Evelyn catches up with Rayona, Rayona is looking out at the yellow raft, hoping she can forget her troubles if she stares hard enough. Evelyn says nothing, but Rayona tells her the whole story. When she is finished, Rayona feels as if a burden has been lifted from her. Evelyn decides that Rayona needs to go home, and that she and Sky are going to drive Rayona there. After his initial surprise when Evelyn and Rayona arrive at the gas station to pick him up, Sky closes up the gas station and gets ready to go. Rayona packs her clothes in a case that Evelyn gives her, and she takes the videos from Village Video. Rayona knows that there is an Indian rodeo in the nearby town of Havre that day and thinks that might be a good place to look for her mother.

As soon as they get to the rodeo, Rayona sees Foxy. Foxy is, as usual, quite rude to Rayona and immediately antagonizes Evelyn, who reacts with hostility. Sky and Evelyn look for seats in the bleachers and leave Rayona and Foxy to talk. Foxy is supposed to be in the rodeo, riding a horse belonging to Dayton, Christine's boyfriend. Foxy, however, is much too drunk to ride, so he tells Rayona to ride for him and flashes a knife to make sure she obeys. To make sure no one knows Rayona is a girl, Foxy lends her his hat and jacket. As Rayona is heading over to the stock pens, she sees Annabelle. Annabelle is outraged when she learns Foxy has been drinking. Rayona thinks to herself that her mother must have looked like Annabelle when she was young. Rayona is reminded of Ellen, but Ellen does not compare to Annabelle.

Rayona climbs onto the horse and spends a nervous moment in the pen before her ride begins. Babe, the horse, throws her three times in one minute, but Rayona keeps getting back on with tenacious determination. By the end of the minute both girl and horse are exhausted. After the ride, Rayona feels changed. Bearpaw Lake and the people she has worked with for the past few weeks seem very far away. Everyone is very impressed by Rayona's bravery in the rodeo. Annabelle calls Rayona "insane," but in a notably friendly tone. When the awards are given out at the end of the day, Rayona—or rather, Foxy—is given a special prize: the "hard-luck buckle." When Rayona gets up to claim her award, she notices everyone looking closely at her. She takes off her hat and jacket, and from across the arena, Evelyn starts cheering for her. Soon, everyone else cheers as well.

ANALYSIS: CHAPTER 7

When Rayona returns to the lake to stare at the yellow raft, she longs one last time to escape her troubles, then bids her fantasy life farewell. Rayona feels that if she stares at the raft long enough it "will launch [her] out of [her] present troubles." This raft is the gateway to the life Rayona has been trying to live, and is the site of her most recent realizations. First the raft is the place where she drifts from Father Tom and breaks the last bond to her old life, and then it is where she first sees Ellen, who lives the life Rayona wants. Rayona is now, however, unable to lose her troubles in such fantasies because Evelyn, who knows that Rayona's world is only an illusion, is standing right behind her. Rayona idealizes Ellen's life, but she nevertheless feels that something took "a weight off" when she confesses her story to Evelyn. When Rayona plunges back into reality she no longer has to bear the burden of sustaining a lie and risking exposure as a fraud. Rayona feels real for the first time in months.

Rayona's first encounter with her old life is with Foxy, whom she sees at the rodeo. This encounter is the worst possible beginning to Rayona's reunion with her past, as Foxy is the cruelest of all the young people on the reservation, but Evelyn gives Rayona the power and confidence to deal with Foxy. Evelyn motivates Rayona to stand up for herself not by connecting her to some fantasy but by showing Rayona that she cares about and supports her. In this way, Evelyn fills in a gap left by Christine, who has never really bothered to act as her daughter's ally.

In any case, Rayona ends up on the back of the wild horse, and her perseverance in staying on the horse is symbolic of her new attempt to live the life she has been given. Riding the horse is a liberating experience for Rayona because it is something real, an experience that is hers and under her control alone. It is true that she is disguised as a boy for her ride, but this temporary transformation allows her to escape from her idealistic self to a more realistic version of herself. In other words, the identity she assumes in the rodeo is much more relevant to her life than the identity she dreams up for herself, and it still liberates her to some degree. By riding, Rayona gains the acceptance and admiration of many of the people in the arena. She gains this admiration by being her real self, not her fantasy self.

CHAPTER 8

SUMMARY: CHAPTER 8

As Rayona steps off of the awards platform, she sees Foxy glowering angrily at her. Rayona also sees Father Tom heading her way. A heavyset, mixed-blood cowboy comes up to Rayona, and the man turns out to be Dayton, Christine's sometime boyfriend and the owner of the horse Rayona has just ridden. Father Tom sidles up and acts as if he is not surprised to see Rayona. Sky and Evelyn arrive, and Rayona introduces them to the others as friends from Bearpaw Lake State Park. The mention of the park startles Father Tom. Annabelle also shows up, and although Rayona hesitates to introduce her as a friend, Annabelle smiles and does not object to the term.

Meanwhile, Evelyn has locked eyes with Father Tom. He realizes Evelyn knows about his dealings with Rayona, and he shrinks abashedly away into the crowd. Dayton agrees to take Rayona home, so Rayona goes with Evelyn and Sky to get her things from the car. Once there, Rayona presents Evelyn with the blanket from the park that she had saved for the older woman. They say goodbye, and Evelyn and Sky ride off. Foxy is still furious, but as he starts toward Rayona, Annabelle intercepts him.

On the way back to Dayton's ranch, Rayona finds out that Dayton was good friends with her uncle, Lee. When they arrive, Christine is both surprised and furious to see Rayona. Christine talks as if Rayona has greatly wronged her, pointing out how sick she has been and chastising Rayona for running away and worrying everybody. Rayona fires back, and the two sling insults at each other until Dayton herds them inside. They sit down in front of the television and watch the local news coverage of the rodeo. Rayona is a major feature, and Christine is amazed to learn that Rayona rode. After the news, an evangelical religious program comes on and everyone goes to bed.

Rayona wakes up the next morning stiff from her rodeo escapade. As she dresses, she sees the horse from the rodeo out in the yard. Rayona recalls Dayton mentioning that once one has broken a horse one can ride it, so she goes outside and hops on Babe. The horse has other plans, however, and tosses Rayona over the fence.

Christine comes outside, and she and Rayona begin talking. Christine explains how she lost her religious faith and gazes at Rayona the same way Rayona gazes at the yellow raft the day before. Christine says she lost her faith because of a letter supposedly from the Virgin Mary. There were all sorts of rumors about the letter: the pope was going to open it in 1960, and as a consequence either the world would end or Communist Russia would be converted. Christine had studied the apocalyptic passages in the Bible as preparation for the end of the world, but when nothing happened, she had become confused. Upon asking one of the sisters at the mission school why nothing had happened, the only answer she had received was that it was a "mystery."

ANALYSIS: CHAPTER 8
Chapter 8 opens with a seemingly out-of-place reference to the old western TV show the "Late Show," a piece of pop culture that Dorris uses to provide parallels to the events of his novel. Rayona men-

tions that in episodes of the "Late Show" everything turns out all right in the end and that the good guy always escapes through some miraculous event that gets him out of whatever trouble he has been facing. Rayona's experience at the rodeo is akin to these miraculous events from the "Late Show." Rayona's performance in the rodeo is unexpected and suddenly makes things seem to turn out well for her. As an ending to Rayona's section of the novel, the rodeo ride is something of a deus ex machina—a literary term for an unexpected event or object that suddenly appears and provides a contrived solution to a seemingly unsolvable situation.

Though the rodeo performance does bring Rayona some of the acceptance she has been seeking, it does not solve all of her problems, and Dorris leaves some loose ends for the rest of the novel to pick up and resolve. Even after the rodeo, Rayona's relationship with her mother is still distant and contentious. When Rayona arrives at Dayton's house, for example, Christine's reaction is not what one might expect from a mother who has lost track of her daughter for several months. Christine is angry, and her anger provokes anger in Rayona. To Rayona, her mother's unwelcoming attitude is irrational, selfish, and stupid. Rayona's tone in this section gives another negative impression of Christine. In later parts of the novel we see this mother-daughter relationship revisited from a different perspective—Christine's—at which point we begin to see more clearly the causes of Rayona and Christine's misunderstandings. For now, however, only Rayona's bitterness is visible.

Christine is more courteous to Rayona the morning after the rodeo, and Dorris begins to reveal the many hopes and dreams she pins on her daughter. Christine tells Rayona the story of a part of her life, and Rayona notes that the expression on her mother's face is much like her own expression when upon looking at the yellow raft the day before. Much as the raft represents an idealized fantasy life for Rayona, Rayona represents the same thing for Christine. Christine goes on to tell Rayona a confessional story about her loss of faith, much as Rayona tells Evelyn a confessional story the day before, and the parallels between these two confessions suggest that Christine may get the same relief from talking to her daughter as Rayona does from talking to Evelyn.

CHAPTER 9

SUMMARY: CHAPTER 9

This chapter marks the start of the second part of the novel, and the narrative voice switches from Rayona to Christine and from the present tense to the past.

Christine's narrative begins immediately after the time Christine expected the world to end. Christine regrets that she missed a party while getting ready for the apocalypse that never came and vows to never miss another party. Christine's brother, Lee, is the best-looking boy on the reservation, but Christine does not consider herself attractive at all. She wonders if she and Lee have the same father, but Aunt Ida never tells them. Ida does not let Christine and Lee call her "mom" because she was never married.

Lee hangs around with Christine throughout grade school. Christine is the toughest kid in her class, so the boys always send her out on dares, which she accepts every time. One day, however, they dare Christine to cross a natural bridge of stone that runs high over a stream. She is almost across when she freezes with fear, paralyzed until Lee comes and pulls her across. When the two walk down the ridge, Christine makes a mental list of things she should never again dare to do.

When Christine is a sophomore and Lee is thirteen, a child of mixed heritage named Dayton Nickles moves to the reservation. Dayton becomes Lee's shadow, following him everywhere. By this time, Christine is popular among her peers, and other girls in her class go to her when they want to learn about making out. One day, Christine is in her room and catches Dayton looking at her from the next room. Taking this look as a sign of Dayton's interest, Christine becomes attracted to Dayton. During a powwow the next April, Christine takes Dayton out to a field and tries to seduce him. They begin kissing, but Dayton pulls away, telling Christine he thinks of her as a sister. Christine is furious. Dayton and Christine have a falling-out, and Lee is torn between them.

Lee is an excellent rider and becomes a rodeo star. However, Aunt Ida refuses to allow Lee to make riding his profession. Christine can tell that Ida has other plans for Lee, but she does not know what they are. Some people claim that Lee will one day be regarded as the Indian JFK because he is so smart and handsome.

After she graduates from high school Christine gets a job with the tribal council and constantly goes out with boys. One night Christine takes a road trip to North Dakota with Diamond, a young man who already has two children, and they stay there for two weeks. When Christine comes home, Ida is angry with her because Diamond's mother has complained to Ida that Christine is preventing her from seeing her grandchildren. Christine moves out of Ida's house and goes to live with Pauline, Ida's sister.

At the end of their high school careers, Lee and Dayton become active in the militant "Red Power" movement. Christine disapproves of Lee's behavior and confronts him at a general store one day. Christine goes to Aunt Ida to tell her that Lee is acting strange, but Ida tells her that Lee is fine and knows what he is doing. Christine leaves the house, feeling forgotten.

ANALYSIS: CHAPTER 9

This new section grows out of the story Christine is telling Rayona at the end of the previous chapter, and it is unclear whether she is telling the story out loud or if the novel has begun to chart Christine's inner thoughts. Certainly, this section is more than just Christine telling a lengthy anecdote, and just as Rayona has done with her confession to Evelyn, Christine is now getting her own story out into the open. Unlike her daughter, however, Christine has the benefit of perspective, and this perspective is indicated by the fact that she uses the past tense (whereas Rayona uses the present tense). Christine, unlike Rayona, is distant enough from her story that she has to look back on it rather than narrate it as it occurs.

This chapter gives us a different perspective on the same reality we have been shown through Rayona's eyes. Whereas Rayona always thinks of her mother as being attractive, we learn here that Christine never thought herself pretty. Because we have two equally subjective viewpoints, it is unclear whether Rayona's admiration of her mother's beauty is truly deserved or just another one of Rayona's idealizations. Conversely, it is unclear whether Christine is correct in thinking she is unattractive or if this perspective merely reflects her low opinion of herself as a person.

Christine begins her narrative by situating us in her era, the 1960s, and Dorris steeps the story in the culture of the 1960s to help us follow Christine's story. Christine lingers on the idea of patriotism for the first few paragraphs, mentioning how important "respect for the red, white, and blue" was for people living on the reservation. Later, Christine mentions many of the popular songs of her day, which she hears on the radio program "The Teen Beat." Because the songs she mentions are still familiar tunes, these references allow us to get some feel for the period. Christine also mentions some well-known political events and trends, all of which plant Christine's story firmly in the 1960s without making it feel unfamiliar to a contemporary reader.

Another interesting aspect of the beginning of Christine's story is the way it weaves into Rayona's narrative and elaborates on some of the details Rayona leaves unexplained. People who are only minor characters in Rayona's story, such as Lee and Dayton, are suddenly more prominent and are given more depth. The origins of several details Rayona mentions in passing are now fully explained, such as the notebook Rayona finds in Christine's room in which Christine tries pairing her name with different boys' last names. In this chapter we get to see the origin of attitudes and trends that are part of Christine's life at the beginning of the novel. For example, Pauline's warning to Christine that she will wear herself out echoes the warnings of Charlene, Christine's friend from Seattle. Some of Christine's behavior seems baffling at the beginning of the novel, but by showing the origins of some of her actions, Dorris brings us closer to understanding them.

CHAPTER 10

SUMMARY: CHAPTER 10

The Vietnam War has begun, and Christine asks Dayton what his draft classification is. Dayton has been classified a "4-A," which means that he cannot be drafted because his father is dead and he is the only son left to his mother. Christine asks Lee what he plans to do after his two years in the military, but he informs her he is not going to enlist, and that he will dodge the draft if he has to. Christine thinks Lee is being a coward and the two get into an argument. The argument ends when Christine slaps Lee across the face.

People wonder whether or not Lee will enlist. Christine gets into an argument about it with Aunt Ida, who supports Lee. One day Christine sees a poster publicizing the tribal elections and knows that Lee will never be elected if he does not join the army, which she explains to Dayton. Dayton and Lee had made plans about Lee eventually running for election to the council, and Dayton recognizes that Christine is right. As a draft-dodger, Lee would never be elected. Dayton commits himself to persuading Lee to enlist.

Lee and Dayton disappear for a few weeks but return the night of the mission's Labor Day bazaar. Lee has cut his hair and enlisted, and he starts hanging around with a new group of friends. Soon Dayton cuts his hair as well, though he clings to his 4-A classification. Christine begins to find the reservation too confining, so she decides to join an employment program in Seattle. She bids a civil farewell to Ida and has a rather drawn-out goodbye with Lee. Lee ships out for boot camp soon after.

Christine makes plenty of new friends in Seattle but her job bores her. She frequently switches jobs and apartments, but never really finds anything she likes. Christine receives two pieces of mail from Lee: a postcard from Hawaii and then a letter from Vietnam. Several months later she gets a letter from Dayton. Lee has been listed as MIA—missing in action. Christine is distraught and dreads getting any more letters.

That night, feeling anxious about Lee, Christine stops in a bar for a drink. It takes a minute for her to realize that everyone in the bar is black. A man in uniform comes over and buys Christine a drink. His name is Corporal Elgin A. Taylor. Christine tells Elgin about Lee, and he puts his arm around her and tells her not to worry. The two go back to Elgin's hotel room together. Being with Elgin is a whole new experience for Christine, and the next morning she asks him never to leave her. He promises that he will not.

ANALYSIS: CHAPTER 10

The deference for the "red, white, and blue" Christine mentions in the previous chapter makes another appearance here. Only when we keep in mind the patriotism that pervades Christine's reservation can we properly understand the ramifications of Lee's desire to dodge the draft. Indeed, after Christine confronts Lee, and the opinions of people on the reservation are split, we see that Lee's enemies claim that he will dodge and his friends claim that he will not. This split gives us a fairly explicit indication that avoiding the military would be poorly received by the entire reservation.

It is unclear why Christine is so anxious to see Lee enlist, and her reasons are in many ways selfish. Her first concern when she learns that Lee may try to dodge the draft is what her friends will say about her. Christine's close association with Lee is a large part of her identity, but we get the impression she enjoys being his sister only when he is popular and well liked. However, we also get the sense that Christine seems to want what is best for Lee. Christine steps up her efforts to persuade Lee to enlist only when she realizes that enlisting would greatly help Lee's future political career. This foresight shows some concern on her part for Lee's future. While Lee's success would also improve Christine's reputation, Christine's ultimate goal seems to be that they succeed as a pair. Regardless of her true intentions, it is clear that Christine ties her identity closely to Lee's.

The wild life Christine lives after graduation is another part of her search for identity. She experiences a switch in personalities from a prudish girl obsessed with the alleged end of the world to a popular social butterfly who never misses a party. This party-girl image Christine adopts causes problems in her relationship with Ida, in essence weakening Christine's identity as a daughter. Christine feels that there is something special waiting for her in the big city, so she goes to Seattle to find it. The jobs she gets are unexciting, however, and none of them provides her with a satisfactory identity to replace the one she has left behind. Although she has shed the discipline and restrictions of life on the reservation, Christine has also lost the support her family provided, and her life feels empty because she is unable to replace this love and support.

When Lee is reported as missing in action, Christine loses one of her last bastions of family love and support. Soon after receiving the news of Lee's disappearance, however, she meets Elgin. After they spend the night together, Christine makes Elgin a part of her identity, a kind of replacement for Lee, who is far away and possibly dead. Elgin becomes a new anchor for Christine, someone who will stay with her, provide her comfort, and validate her existence.

CHAPTER 11

SUMMARY: CHAPTER 11

Christine is a changed woman after her encounter with Elgin. She waits impatiently for Elgin's discharge from the military. When that day comes, Elgin comes home late but Christine is just as glad to see him. They spend a passionate few weeks in Tacoma, living off of Elgin's savings and spending all of their time together. Christine decides she wants a child and stops using birth control. One day, she and Elgin make love in Point Defiance Park and Christine immediately knows she is pregnant. She tells Elgin and he proposes to her.

Elgin's money begins to run low, so he gets a job with the post office. Christine stops drinking and smoking and starts going to bed early. She goes back to her job on an assembly line making black boxes for airplanes. Christine is starting to look quite pregnant, and she wonders when she and Elgin will get married. They decide to have their wedding ceremony at a courthouse and then go to a club afterward. Everyone at the club is enthusiastic when they find out Elgin and Christine are newlyweds. On the walk home, Christine can feel Elgin drawing away from her, but her fears are allayed when he carries her the last two blocks to their hotel.

Christine writes a letter to Aunt Ida to tell her about the marriage but gets no reply. Elgin starts coming home later and later. When Christine yells at Elgin and accuses him of seeing someone else, she suddenly realizes that she sounds just like a woman that one of her former boyfriends deserted to date her. Elgin disappears for three days. When he returns, Christine does not ask where he has been. One morning, a week past her due date, Christine receives a letter from Dayton stating that Lee is dead. Christine's water breaks and she takes a taxi to the hospital, putting Dayton's letter in the back of her mind.

Elgin does not show up at the hospital. Christine has some difficulty dealing with the discomfort of childbirth but makes it through. She was planning to name the baby Raymond, but the baby is a girl. When Elgin shows up, he wants to name the baby Diane after his mother, but Christine comes up with "Rayona." Rayona's middle name becomes Diane. Christine refuses to let the nurses put Rayona in a nursery, so they give her a private room.

Things are good between Elgin and Christine after Rayona is born, but soon Elgin again begins to stay out later and later. When Rayona is nine months old, Christine goes back to work and finds a place of her own. After that, Elgin calls from time to time, claiming he wants to start over. Christine listens to him at times, and at other times does not.

ANALYSIS: CHAPTER 11

Christine is deliriously happy to find someone who appreciates and loves her, and at first her relationship with Elgin overwhelms even the affection she has known on the reservation. Her new identity as

Elgin's girlfriend gives Christine a place and a kind of acceptance she has never felt before. In this regard, Christine's relationship with Elgin is analogous to Rayona's relationship with Father Tom. In both cases, an isolated and lonely individual finds someone willing to shower attention on her. However, both Rayona and Christine end up having negative experiences with the men they come to trust. The relationship between Rayona and Father Tom and the relationship between Christine and Elgin clearly have their differences, in terms of the level of emotion and commitment involved, the outcome, and the extent to which each party is invested in the relationship. However, both relationships are part of the same search, in which a young woman who can no longer turn to her family tries to find other people to love and accept her.

Christine decides she wants to augment the identity that Elgin provides her by becoming a mother, and every time her relationship with Elgin deepens, Christine temporarily finds satisfaction in her life. Once Christine becomes pregnant and betrothed to Elgin, she is content to go back to one of the jobs she had previously thought was too boring. Her menial job, which was previously unbearably tedious, is now suffused with greater meaning because it represents a means to support her child. Just like Rayona, however, Christine can believe in her fictionalized life only if other people do the same. On the evening of her wedding, Christine enjoys telling all the people at the club that she and Elgin are newly married. Just as Rayona finds an identity by getting Sky and Evelyn to believe in her fictional life, Christine reaffirms her identity as a wife and mother-to-be by publicly proclaiming her marriage. Each believes that having others know about her life, whether real or fictional, validates her identity.

Christine makes a major leap in understanding herself after Elgin begins repeatedly staying out late at night, and her rosy view of her life gives way to unflattering comparisons to women she has known in the past. Feeling abandoned by Elgin, Christine suddenly realizes how similar she is to the nagging wives of men with whom she used to have affairs, women whom she always disparaged. Suddenly seeing things from the viewpoint of these lonely wives makes Christine reevaluate herself and reinforces her suspicion that Elgin is cheating on her. Christine begins trying to keep Elgin close to her and simultaneously gains perspective on the somewhat promiscuous lifestyle she had been leading. This sudden self-awareness demonstrates how Christine has changed in only a few months. Becoming pregnant has made her cautious, thoughtful, and unusually responsible and has made her begin looking at herself in a new light.

CHAPTER 12

SUMMARY: CHAPTER 12

Lee's corpse is finally delivered to the reservation, and Christine takes Rayona to the funeral. Christine drives her new car, a Volaré, through a snowstorm late at night. At one point during the drive, Christine, in a fit of snow blindness, thinks she sees Lee standing by the side of the road, halfway up a golden staircase and holding his hand out for her. Focused on this vision, Christine skids the car and spins off the road. After changing Rayona's diaper and feeding her in the car, Christine starts off again toward the reservation.

By the time Christine and Rayona arrive, Lee's body is lying in wait at Aunt Ida's house. When Christine sees Ida, she is struck by the similarities between Ida and Rayona. Many people attend Lee's wake, but Dayton is not among them. Christine is ready to forgive Dayton for not going to war, but she soon realizes that some of the people on the reservation blame her for Lee's death. Christine asks Ida where she can put Rayona to sleep. For the first time Ida shows some affection to Rayona.

Lee's funeral is the next day, and Father Hurlburt stops by to lead everyone to the church. Christine has not been to church once since the world failed to end years before, so she stands at the back. Christine sees Dayton sitting in the pews, and she flashes her wedding ring at him as he is leaving. As it is winter, the ground is too hard to bury Lee, so the mourners take handfuls of potting soil to throw on the casket. When they are finished, Ida cleans off the dirt and shakes cedar out onto the casket in a six-pointed pattern, in the center of which she places Lee's championship buckle. The only person who does not throw her dirt is Christine, who stands petrified and unable to move. Finally, Dayton grabs Christine's wrist and tells her she must bury Lee. When Dayton lets go of Christine's arm, she is able to move again and throws dirt on the coffin.

There is a get-together at Pauline's, but Christine and Dayton skip it and go to dinner in town instead. They order food but do not talk much. Christine brags about her life in Seattle. Later, the veterans hold an honor ceremony for Lee at the mission gym. Willard Pretty Dog, one of the veterans, pulls Ida into a dance. Chris-

tine dances with Vernon, another veteran, and Dayton dances with baby Rayona.

ANALYSIS: CHAPTER 12

Despite Christine's disillusionment with religion, in this chapter we see her fall back on her faith as a support, and religion takes on a new credibility in the novel. As she is driving through the snowstorm to the funeral, Christine prays for protection against skidding on the icy road. Unlike her previous religious experiences, which were as a member of an organized religious group, Christine's prayer exhibits a personal faith. Out on the snowy road, Christine does not have to deal with religious dogma and prays directly to God without an intermediary. This is the first time we see personal, purified religious faith in the novel. Rayona's dealings with the church, for instance, actually have very little to do with God and are more style than substance. The God Squad and other catchphrases of Father Tom's had characterized religion in Rayona's section more than had any actual religious faith. Christine's faith as her car skids out of control, however, is a purer, more meaningful version of religion than we have previously seen.

Christine's vision of Lee clearly has religious overtones, but its meaning is open to interpretation and gives all of the events surrounding the vision a mysterious feel. The image of Lee climbing a flight of golden stairs is an unmistakable symbol of him ascending to heaven. However, the fact that Lee is holding out his hand toward Christine is intriguing, as Lee seems to be indicating that he wants Christine to follow him. This vision could mean that Christine is going to die soon, literally following Lee up the golden staircase. It could also, however, indicate that Christine is meant to follow Lee in some other way, to more closely emulate Lee's life. The vagueness of this vision leads to a car accident of equally ambiguous nature. The skid appears to be an accident, but it can also be read as a passive suicide attempt, since Christine says she "let [the world] go with no regrets." Even so, as she spins off the road Christine throws herself over Rayona to keep her baby from flying out of the car. This gesture is clearly protective, and signifies that Christine cares enough about Rayona to keep from seizing an opportunity to end her life and truly follow Lee.

Earlier we encounter the possibility that Christine wanted Lee to join the army at least partly out of concern for her own reputation, and now we see this selfishness backfire. At Lee's wake, Christine sees that Lee's enlistment has, ironically, actually been detrimental to her reputation, as many people on the reservation blame her for Lee's death. Christine's reaction to this blame is two-fold. She comes to the reservation ready to forgive Dayton for dodging the draft and to play the part of the grieving but kind sister. When she realizes that people blame her, Christine becomes angry at Dayton and Ida, a reaction that seems to indicate that Christine's primary interest is still her own reputation. However, Christine's emotional state at Lee's funeral shows that her grief is very real. While the other mourners are sad, they are at least able to contribute to Lee's burial, but Christine is too stricken with grief to throw her handful of dirt onto Lee's coffin. She does not want to forget Lee and is unable to make this final gesture until Dayton forces her to. For Christine, Lee is still only halfway up the golden steps.

Dayton finally forces Christine to accept the reality of Lee's death and let go of his memory. Now that Lee is gone, Christine's best and clearest memories of him are through Dayton. Christine and Dayton share a connection after Lee's death that is as strong as the one they shared over Lee's future when he was still alive. Lee was originally a source of competition for Christine and Dayton, but now their shared memories of him bring them closer together.

CHAPTER 13

SUMMARY: CHAPTER 13

> *Rayona gave me something to be, made me like other*
> *women with children. I was nobody's regular*
> *daughter, nobody's sister, usually nobody's wife, but I*
> *was her mother full time.*
>
> (See QUOTATIONS, p. 75)

Christine and Rayona leave the reservation, and Christine takes her time driving home. They get back to Seattle on a Saturday night and Christine wants to go out but cannot find a babysitter. Undeterred, Christine takes Rayona along with her to the Silver Bullet, her usual bar. There, Christine sees Elgin with his arm around a fat woman. Christine catches Elgin's eye, and he comes over to talk. They end up going home together, and Elgin stays for two weeks.

Elgin continues to disappear and reappear in Christine's life, and she takes him back every time. She has other boyfriends, along with friends and jobs, but the only constant in her life is Rayona. Rayona is a very independent child and does things for herself whenever she can.

One day Aunt Ida calls to let Christine know that she is in town and will be staying over. Ida's aunt, Clara, is sick and staying at Indian Health Services. Rayona does not remember Ida so Christine tries to describe her. When Ida arrives, Rayona acts shy for the first time in her life. Ida makes a point of commenting on Christine's conspicuous lack of a husband but is kind to Rayona and even brings a doll for her. That Saturday Ida makes Christine and Rayona accompany her on the bus to Indian Health Services. When they arrive, Ida introduces Christine and Rayona—but especially Rayona—to all the elderly Indians who are waiting around. Clara is glad to see her family, especially Christine, but before long Ida decides it is time for them to leave. Though Christine promises Clara she will come back to the hospital for a longer visit, Clara dies before Christine gets a chance. Ida decides she wants to go back to the reservation, but Christine persuades her to stay for dinner. Ida insists on making most of the dinner herself. When Rayona calls Ida "Grandma," Ida corrects her and tells her to call her "Aunt Ida." Rayona is offended and leaves the kitchen.

Elgin shows up the next day, and promises to be there whenever Christine needs him. In raising Rayona, Christine tries to do a better job than Ida did with her, and for the most part she feels she accomplishes this goal. She gets very angry when Elgin disappoints Rayona by not being around. She loves Rayona but knows she will never have another child. She cannot have Rayona end up the way she did, forgotten because of Lee. She never feels the same as she had that day at Point Defiance, not with Elgin or anyone else.

ANALYSIS: CHAPTER 13

As Christine realizes that being a wife and mother is not enough to solve her problems, she reverts to her old habits and begins to lose control of her life. She does not want anyone other than Elgin but cannot live with him for more than a few weeks at a time. This realization makes her steely and jaded, so she does "what it t[akes] to get by" by going out and meeting new boyfriends. She returns to the more volatile lifestyle she embraces when she first goes to Seattle.

Even Rayona, who had anchored Christine to a stable life, becomes an accessory, a friend Christine can bring along to bars. Christine says that, in retrospect, at this point in her life she knew she was headed in the wrong direction but was too far out of control to see a solution. Indeed, we see her live such a fast-paced life that perspective is difficult for her to gain. The stability she experiences during her pregnancy is gone, as is anything resembling a committed marital relationship with Elgin, and her current instability is even worse than her experiences during her first few months in Seattle. Christine no longer seems to be searching for an identity, and views each new episode in her life as something to tide her over until her next encounter with Elgin.

Christine initially remembers very little about Clara, whom Ida has mentioned before, but never by name. When Christine and Rayona accompany Ida on her visit to the IHS, there is clearly some underlying tension between Ida and Clara, but Christine is unable to get at the root of the conflict. Clara is very glad to see Christine, but Ida cuts their interview short. We get the definite impression that Ida is somehow trying to keep Christine and Clara apart, and this moment foreshadows important revelations in Ida's narrative.

Christine's determination to do a better job raising Rayona than her own mother did raising her gives us a new perspective on what was missing in Christine's childhood, but Christine is careful not to overstep her bounds and try to live an idealized life through Rayona. The fact that Christine is sure to note that she "answered Rayona's questions" shows how much the secrecy pervading her own upbringing had bothered her. Christine does not want Rayona to feel forgotten the way she herself did. Christine's desire to shape a different life for Rayona, however, does not mean that she intends to live vicariously through her. Christine even notes that she does not expect to relive her life through Rayona, not because she does not want to but because she does not think she can. While this remark is in some ways a sign that Christine is defeated, as if she feels too set in her ways to correct her mistakes, it is also an important acknowledgement on Christine's part that Rayona is a separate and unique person. In trying to be a better mother than Ida, Christine hopes to help Rayona avoid derailing her own life.

CHAPTER 14

SUMMARY: CHAPTER 14

> *When I thought back ... I saw my greatest hits, the K-Tel Christine Taylor album.... That was what I amounted to, my big days revolving on the TV screen like Four Seasons titles.*
>
> (See QUOTATIONS, p. 76)

The doctor at Indian Health Services tells Christine that she has worn out her liver and pancreas, and that she has only about six months left to live. Christine's only response is to ask the doctor for a deck of cards. He tells Christine she needs to plan for her daughter, but she persists in asking for cards. The two Native American women in the beds next to Christine are interested in her story. They were in the hospital when Christine was brought in the night before, kicking, screaming, and ridiculously drunk.

Christine knows Rayona is coming to visit but dreads talking to her because she knows her death will have severe consequences for Rayona. When Rayona arrives, Christine braids her hair. Christine is amazed at how little Rayona resembles her and recalls that when she was Rayona's age she was already popular and knew all about boys. When she finishes with Rayona's hair, Christine teaches her a game of cards. Elgin shows up to deliver the Volaré but does not seem to want to talk. Christine wants Elgin to stay for a while, and is furious and disappointed when he leaves. Christine hides her head beneath her sheets, and when she looks up both Elgin and Rayona are gone. Christine steals some nurse's clothes and sneaks out of the hospital. Rayona surprises Christine while she is trying to break into the Volaré. Christine tells Rayona she is going to crash the car and leave Rayona with the money from the insurance settlement, but Rayona decides her mother is bluffing and forces her way into the car. Rayona annoys Christine by guessing her destination, which is Point Defiance in Tacoma. When they arrive, Christine pulls over and tells Rayona to get out. Rayona screams at her and kicks the Volaré. Christine turns the key to leave, but the car is out of gas. Looking at her child, Christine realizes that whatever else she has to do in her life she has to do with Rayona. Deciding she has scared her daughter enough for one day, Christine attempts to cheer Rayona up by kidding with her as they walk to the gas station.

Christine decides to take Rayona to Aunt Ida's because she wants Ida to look after Rayona when she dies. Christine and Rayona go home to pack but there is not much to take. Christine persuades her neighbor, who works at a pharmacy, to send her some painkillers through the mail. Christine wants to leave something for Rayona to have while she is on the reservation, but realizes she has nothing really impressive to give. She then remembers her membership at Village Video. She chooses the movie Christine as one of the rentals because she wants Rayona to remember her as tough, like the car in the movie. They leave the video store and head off to Aunt Ida's.

The Volaré dies about a mile away from Aunt Ida's, and Christine decides that she and Rayona can walk the rest of the way. When they get there, Ida is outside mowing the lawn. She asks Christine for three reasons why she should be glad to see her. Christine knows Ida is happy to see her crawling back. She carefully chooses her first two reasons and tells Ida, "I'm your daughter, your only living child" and "[W]e need someplace to stay." She chooses the first response because it touches on Ida's motherly obligations and reminds her of Lee—a subject that would surely come up later—and the second response because it gives Ida some satisfaction to know that Christine needs her. Christine knows that if she admits she was wrong to defy Ida as her third reason for returning, Ida will take her in and give her anything she needs, but she cannot bring herself to admit her error in front of Rayona. Instead Christine insults her mother and turns back toward the road.

> In school they had taught her all this crap about drinking and how bad it was for you, smoking too, and she was convinced I used more than I did, that I was an alcoholic.

ANALYSIS: CHAPTER 14
For the first time, the events of Christine's story overlap with the events of Rayona's, which gives us a great amount of insight into the two women's different perspectives. Christine's braiding of Rayona's hair, which immediately precedes the game of cards that opens Rayona's narrative, is the prefect metaphor for the narrative structure that Dorris is employing here. A Yellow Raft in Blue Water consists of the stories of three women of different generations, but these three stories all overlap to create one unified structure, just as a braid weaves separate strands together. Dorris uses

the braid as a symbol of this union, and introduces this metaphor at a point in the novel when the connection between the three stories first becomes apparent.

Christine's actions in the hospital, which seem silly, irrational, and selfish from Rayona's point of view, take on a whole new meaning for us when we see them in the larger context of Christine's life, and the disagreements in their stories tell us more about each character. There are small discrepancies between the two versions of the story that make us doubt that either one is the absolute truth and recognize how each character's perspective inevitably shapes how she understands the story. For example, in Christine's version, she tells Elgin to go back to his "little fat girl," but Rayona translates this command as "go back to your little black girl." Considering Christine's earlier reference to Elgin's flirtation with a fat woman, her version seems the more accurate. From this simple discrepancy, therefore, we can see that Rayona often sees a racial issue where there is none, which in turn tells us more about how Rayona's mixed heritage has heightened her sensitivity to the issue of race.

These misunderstandings between mother and daughter take on a tragic tone later in the chapter. We know Christine has just found out that she has only a few months to live, but Rayona and Elgin are unaware of this fact and think Christine is just being melodramatic. At the end of the chapter, the consequences of Christine's behavior expand to her relationship with Ida as well. Christine continues to keep her fatal illness a secret, even though, if told, it would smooth out her relationship with both Ida and Rayona. Instead, Christine remains silent and leaves Rayona feeling abandoned and Ida feeling confused and irritated. Christine's behavior is motivated by her desire to find Rayona a home, but she never lets anyone know her plans or motives. Therefore, what seems natural and right to Christine frequently seems irrational and selfish to others. Ironically, Christine alienates the two people who should be closest to her at a time when she needs them both the most.

CHAPTER 15

SUMMARY: CHAPTER 15
A truck pulls up next to Christine, and the boy inside offers her a ride. He is Kennedy Cree, better known as Foxy, Pauline's son and Christine's cousin. Christine gets in the truck and they drive off.

Foxy offers to take her to Pauline's house, but Christine is not in the mood for Pauline's self-righteous preaching. Christine asks Foxy if Dayton's mother is still around. She has died, but Dayton still lives on her land in a new house next to her former residence, which is now boarded up. Christine asks Foxy to take her there, and although he has a strange reaction to her mention of Dayton's name, he agrees. He puts in an eight-track of Santana on the car stereo and they drive off.

Christine finds a spare key and lets herself into Dayton's house. The house is very clean and new. Christine is surprised to find a picture of herself on the wall, next to a picture of Dayton's mother and one of Lee and Dayton together. Christine puts her things away and lies down on the couch. When Dayton arrives, she pretends to be asleep, watching him through half-closed lids. When he sees Christine, Dayton nervously files away some papers that are out on his desk. Christine makes a show of waking up, and the two have a very awkward conversation. Christine tries to tell Dayton about her health condition, but does not get very far. Dayton lets her stay. Christine goes to the guest room and takes a long rest.

When Christine wakes up, Dayton is gone, but has left a note saying when he will be back. Christine sets herself to finding the papers Dayton put away so hastily when he saw her on his couch. The papers are not in Dayton's drawers, so Christine searches the rest of the house, and they turn up in a box of detergent in the laundry room. Most of the papers are newspaper clippings that tell a surprising story: Dayton had become a teacher at a public school just outside the reservation, but one of his students had accused him of "improper conduct." Dayton denied all the allegations but was nonetheless sentenced to five years in jail. The papers also contain some Xerox copies of other articles, one about Dayton's mother's death, the other an interview with Dayton just after he was released from jail early for good behavior. In the article, Dayton said he had learned accounting in jail and had gotten a job with the tribe, hoping to leave the past behind him. Christine spends the rest of the day looking around Dayton's house.

When Christine's supply of pills runs low she calls Charlene, her friend in Seattle, who was supposed to send her a refill. Charlene has sent the pills to Aunt Ida's. Christine has Dayton drive her to Ida's during the day, when Rayona will be away at school. Ida is watching her soaps when Christine arrives. They get into an argument and Ida shouts that she never wanted Christine. Christine starts to leave as

Ida tries to call her back. Christine tells Ida just to take care of Rayona, and Ida storms off.

ANALYSIS: CHAPTER 15

Christine's journey to Dayton's house is, in a sense, a return to her childhood. Now that Lee is dead, Dayton is perhaps the only person still alive who shares the same experiences of growing up as Christine does. On the way to Dayton's house, Foxy puts on an eight-track recording of Santana on the truck stereo. Although Foxy does not really recognize the songs, Santana is of Christine's era and returns her to her childhood. Christine's reaction to this small bit of pop culture indicates that part of her still longs for the era of her childhood. The Santana song is an apt anthem for the ride to Dayton's house, since visiting Dayton is, for Christine, a journey into the past.

When Christine arrives at Dayton's house, however, she is struck by how new everything looks, and the house becomes a hopeful symbol of new beginnings. At this point, Dayton's house is practically the only thing in the novel that has a feeling of novelty. Everything on the reservation, as well as everything Christine has encountered in Seattle, has been old, used, and worn out. Dayton's shiny new house represents the possibility and allure of starting anew. Even so, this monument to newness stands next to Dayton's mother's boarded-up residence, an inescapable reminder of the past. The old house remind us that, like Christine, Dayton is burdened by his past and plagued by bad memories that remain even after he has tried to build a new life for himself. There is, however, sometimes a good side to holding on to the past, and although Christine is a portion of Dayton's past, he does not mind her staying in his house. Likewise, the pictures Dayton keeps on his wall clearly demonstrate that there are in fact some memories he wishes to preserve.

The final scene of the chapter is another case of confrontation brought on by misunderstanding. As is the case with Christine and Rayona, the misunderstanding between Christine and Ida goes both ways. Although Christine is rude and combative, Ida refuses to listen to Christine and does not give her a chance to explain. We later come to understand Ida's wild remarks better when we hear her own story, but at this point we can see only how bruising her remarks are to Christine. Because we hear Ida's words through Christine's ears, we are able to interpret them only from Christine's perspective.

When Ida says she never wanted Christine, she assumes that Ida means she never wanted Christine as a daughter. As we learn later, however, this is only partly true, and the remark becomes more understandable when seen in context. Caught up in the confusion of the moment, Ida retreats "into a place [Christine] couldn't see." Although Christine means these words literally, they could also refer to events she does not know of in Ida's life, and it is because Christine cannot see this place that she cannot understand her supposed mother.

CHAPTER 16

SUMMARY: CHAPTER 16

Dayton and Christine settle into the routine of an "old married couple." Christine stays on Dayton's land almost all of the time. There are certain topics she avoids in her conversations with Dayton: her health, Elgin, and Rayona. One day Father Hurlburt comes to Dayton's house with Aunt Ida. Ida tells Christine that Rayona disappeared a few days earlier. Ida adds that Father Tom thinks that Rayona has gone back to Seattle, and that it is all for the best. Ida tells Christine to call if she needs her and leaves. After Ida's visit, Christine thinks and worries about Rayona constantly. In her anxiety, she tells Dayton all about Rayona.

Foxy comes by in early July to take Dayton and Babe, Dayton's wild horse, to a rodeo. Dayton says he will be gone for the night but will be back the following evening. Christine spends the night quiet and alone. She does not watch television or listen to the radio, but just sits in a chair as the night passes. The next day goes by relatively quickly and Dayton arrives earlier than expected. Christine wants to hear all about the rodeo. She takes some pills so that the pain from her illness will not make her act strangely, then goes outside. Christine thinks she sees Lee stepping toward her from the truck, but the figure turns into Rayona. The pills have made Christine delirious and she does not know how to react. She and Rayona get into a fight, but Dayton shoos them inside. They all sit down and watch the local news coverage of the rodeo on television, but Christine sees Lee instead of Rayona on the horse. Christine says she has to go to bed and Dayton walks her to her room. During the night, Dayton comes into Christine's room and she snuggles up against him. He is gone the next morning. Walking about after her rest, Christine realizes that her pain feels different because she is now able to control it. She walks out to Babe's corral, part of her usual morning ritual, and finds Rayona asleep on the ground. Christine sits down and hugs her daughter.

Christine, Dayton, and Rayona begin to do a lot of things together. One night, Dayton rents a VCR and Rayona surprises him by pulling out Christine and Little Big Man. They watch both movies. The night before Christine's birthday, they invite Aunt Ida over for dinner. Ida is actually nice and compliments everything. Ida has brought over Christine's high school yearbook and everyone gathers around to have a look. They all then sit down to watch Knots Landing, one of Ida's shows.

Dayton fixes the Volaré and Christine teaches Rayona to drive. Dayton sees an ad in the newspaper requesting a stud horse and decides to take Babe over. Rayona wants to come as well, so Dayton takes her with him. Just after Rayona and Dayton leave, Father Tom shows up at Dayton's house, but Christine is not sure who he is. He is very friendly and gives Christine a bottle of the painkillers she needs, telling her to ask him if she needs any more. Christine worried only a few days earlier that her supply was running low and that she would need to check back into the hospital if it ran out. Christine finally remembers out loud that Ida had in fact mentioned Father Tom. Father Tom's friendliness suddenly disappears and he leaves abruptly.

Later, after Dayton and Rayona return, Rayona starts learning to drive a stick-shift, using Dayton's truck for practice. Christine decides that she and Rayona should go to pick up Babe themselves. Dayton protests, but Christine is insistent. Rayona drives and tells her mother about some of her friends from Bearpaw Lake. They stop at a diner in Havre for breakfast. When Christine goes to the bathroom to wash her hands, her rings slip off of her fingers, which have grown thin because of her illness. She wraps the rings individually to give to the people in her life: the abalone ring for Ida, the roadrunner for Dayton, and the gold wedding ring for Elgin. The last ring, the silver turtle, she brings out and gives to Rayona. Rayona pays for breakfast with some of the money she made at Bearpaw Lake. A little torn piece of paper slips out of her wallet. Rayona looks at it briefly and then throws it away. When Christine and Rayona arrive to pick up Babe, the horse does not want to leave. The rancher says that his horse and Babe fell in love, and that he has never seen anything like it before.

ANALYSIS: CHAPTER 16

Christine and Rayona's reunion is another instance of misunderstanding between mother and daughter. In her version of the story, Rayona says that she is confused and offended by the reception she receives from her mother after she returns from several months' absence. In this chapter, however, we see the same scene from Christine's point of view. Whereas Rayona interprets Christine's surprise as unhappiness to see her, we learn here that Christine's odd behavior is at least partly due to the pills she takes. In fact, it becomes apparent that Christine is so affected by painkillers that she is incapable of even sorting out her own thoughts and leaves a lot of her own dialogue out of her narrative, as if she does not know or understand what she is saying herself. Instead, she has only the haziest notion of what occurs when she is reunited with Rayona, and sums up the whole encounter in a few brief points.

Christine's narrative continues for a little while beyond the point where Rayona's story leaves off, and the significance of the videos they rent in Seattle finally becomes clear. The movies, Christine, and Little Big Man have been Rayona's companions ever since her departure from Seattle, and for one reason or another she has always taken them with her. It turns out that Christine did not originally rent the videos to impress her friends on the reservation, but because she wanted to leave Rayona something by which to remember her. To some extent, the videos serve that purpose, and, in her own narrative, Rayona remembers her mother every time she thinks of the videos. For the most part, however, the videos in Rayona do not rouse the kinds of memories for which Christine is hoping: every time Rayona mentions the videos, she thinks of how silly it was for Christine to have rented them. When mother and daughter finally get a chance to watch the videos together, however, the movies finally serve their intended purpose, creating a bond between Christine and Rayona.

Rayona overcomes another emotional hurdle a few weeks later when she is eating breakfast with her mother in the diner. Christine only sees a small piece of paper fall out of Rayona's wallet, which Rayona takes a short look at and then throws away. We can guess, however, that the little piece of paper is the letter Rayona had found at Bearpaw Lake, an integral part of the fantasy life Rayona had created for herself and of the lies she had told to Sky and Evelyn. In throwing the letter away, Rayona demonstrates that she no longer needs this fantasy life to sustain her. She is finally satisfied with her real family and life and does not want to imagine her mother as being any other way than she actually is. In essence, Rayona's discarding of the letter is a gesture of pride in her family and herself, and an end to her days of coveting other people's lives.

CHAPTER 17

SUMMARY: CHAPTER 17

Ida's narrative begins with an explanation of the context of her life. Ida describes her life as one characterized by resentment, and says that if she could begin her life again, she would learn how to say "No." Ida tells us that she goes through her story daily, and though she may one day tell her tale to Rayona, no one realizes that it is she, Ida, whose life truly drives the story of her family.

When Ida begins her story, her mother is sick and her aunt, Clara, has just arrived to take care of her. Clara fascinates Ida, who watches her aunt unpack while Ida's sister, Pauline, runs to get their father. Ida is troubled when she catches herself thinking that her mother's sickness might be a good thing because it prompted Clara's arrival. Clara has come at the insistence of Ida's mother and over the objections of Ida's father, Lecon. Lecon does not want Clara to come because he worries that other people on the reservation will shame him for wearing out his wife and not being able to care for her himself. Ida offered to drop out of school to care for her mother, but her father would not allow that either. Finally, Ida's mother suggested that they tell everyone Clara was homeless and needed somewhere to stay. Ida's father agreed because he knew the community would esteem them for taking in a homeless woman. Now that Clara has actually arrived, however, Ida's father has begun to act strangely.

Ida is very friendly toward Clara, giving her gifts and taking her to a secret place on the roof to talk. Ida even tells Clara her secrets, such as her crush on Willard Pretty Dog, a boy in her class. Ida begins to do better in school because Clara helps her with her studies. Lecon is very friendly to Clara, doing chores for her and buying her gifts, but Pauline does not seem to like Clara and spends most of her time working with the nuns at the mission. Pauline owns a colorful beaded rosary and is extremely proud of it. However, when Clara comments that the beads of the rosary are most likely scrap beads left over from other regular rosaries, Pauline grows upset and throws the rosary away.

One night, just before Christmas, Ida returns home to find her mother and Clara in tears. Clara is dressed for travel and refuses to tell Ida what has happened unless Ida promises not to hate her. Ida promises and Clara tells her that she is pregnant by Lecon. That night Ida hears her mother, Lecon, and Clara arguing. Ida's mother wants Clara to leave her house and her imminent departure mortifies Lecon because it will shame the family. To make things worse, Clara has told some of the men on the reservation that a baby is due at Lecon's house. Clara points out that she has not said whose child it is, and that no one will suspect Lecon. Clara tells Ida's parents about Ida's crush on Willard Pretty Dog and says they could always claim it was Ida's baby. Ida's mother agrees to let Clara stay, but only if Ida agrees. Before her parents can even ask, Ida has already walked into the room and consented.

Ida's family calls over the new priest at the mission, Father Hurlburt, who has a reputation for secrecy among the people at the reservation. They tell him that a drifter has raped Clara and that there is now only one way for them to preserve the family's honor. Father Hurlburt is reluctant to go along but eventually acquiesces. He knows a motherhouse in Colorado where Clara and Ida can go to wait out Clara's pregnancy. Clara tells Ida not to be sad, because they will have a lot of fun in Colorado.

ANALYSIS: CHAPTER 17

Ida's story begins to explain some of her quirks, which we have seen in Rayona's and Christine's narratives. As with the understanding we gain from combining perspectives on the frequent confrontations between Christine and Rayona, many of the cold and absurd things that Ida does make sense once we are able to look inside her head. Ida begins her story by mentioning her resentment, and everyone who knows her in the other stories is aware of this trait's outward manifestations. In Rayona's and Christine's stories, Ida is almost always grumpy and cold; we now see that this exterior aloofness is due to Ida's bitterness toward the friends and family who have used her. Ida also alludes to the fact that she has reasons for her resentment other than Clara, but she leaves this part of her story for later.

Another of Ida's oddities explained in this chapter is her refusal to speak English except when absolutely necessary, which we now understand as Ida's way of retaining some control over the world around her. "Indian," as Rayona calls it, is the language that has molded Ida's life, and is the language in which she can express herself most explicitly. When she is speaking Indian, Ida is in a realm that she can control, and her desire to face the world on her own terms, through her own language, is especially understandable in the context of the first paragraph of her story. Ida says that if she could live her life differently, she would do it by saying "No" more often, which gives us the sense that Ida feels she has often yielded to the will of others at the expense of her own goals and desires. By speaking Indian with others, Ida forces them to interact with her on her own terms in a way that she can control.

Ida says that she is the foundation upon which the stories of Christine and Rayona are built, and in her story we do see the beginnings of trends that are passed on to Rayona and Christine. Christine notes earlier how alike Rayona and Ida appear, but their similarities are more than just physical. For example, we find that as a child, Ida is very much like Rayona. In school, Ida is smart but refuses to put any effort into her studies, and forty years later we see Rayona display the same intelligence and the same disregard for the authority of the nuns at the mission school. Additionally, we see in Ida much of the same insecurity about appearances that we seen in both Christine and Rayona, and like Rayona, Ida frequently imagines living someone else's life. When Ida thinks of Willard Pretty Dog, for example, she envisions herself taking on Clara's features and having the type of beauty that will please him.

Father Hurlburt's prominence in Ida's story is somewhat unexpected, and the fact that Christine and Rayona recognize him only as a tangential figure shows how secretive Ida has been about her own life. Based on the earlier chapters, we would never suspect that Father Hurlburt is connected to the story of Ida and her family from the very beginning. This revelation is especially surprising when we consider that Father Hurlburt helps Ida and her family perpetrate the fraud that excuses Clara's pregnancy, which means he is a big part of the one event that sets all three of the novel's stories in motion. That Christine and Rayona are ignorant of Father Hurlburt's role in their lives shows what a thorough job Ida has done in burying her past; even her putative daughter and granddaughter are unaware of the key players in their own histories.

CHAPTER 18

SUMMARY: CHAPTER 18

The nuns at the motherhouse in Denver are very impressed by the story of Clara's rape, and as she embellishes her story more and more the nuns begin to make her out as a saint or martyr. Posing as Clara's sister, Ida pays for their room and board by doing manual labor for the nuns. The nuns want Clara to give up her baby for adoption and become a nun herself. Ida looks forward to returning home, resuming a normal life, and getting a chance to rest. Ida receives one letter from Pauline, on the back of which is scrawled a quick note relating how their parents are fighting and how Pauline hates living at home.

Clara has a baby girl whom the nuns name Christine. When the nuns come to bring Ida the news, she pretends not to speak English well enough to understand, which she has been doing since her arrival at the motherhouse. The nuns explain that she is "Aunt Ida" now. Ida demands to see Clara, and although the nuns object, Ida is unrelenting. Clara tells Ida that she is planning to give Christine up for adoption, but Ida rejects the plan. When Ida threatens to tell the nuns the truth about the baby's father, Clara lets Ida take Christine home and promises that she will soon return home as well.

Father Hurlburt picks Ida up after her bus ride from Colorado. On the ride back to Ida's house, he shows off some of the Indian phrases he has learned. He tells Ida that his grandmother was Native American, and Ida can tell from his appearance that he is telling the truth. Ida realizes that this must be why she saw Father Hurlburt as more than a priest on the night that he paid his first visit to Ida and her family. Father Hurlburt also tells Ida that Pauline is no longer living with their parents because Lecon's drinking has become a problem. When Ida and Father Hurlburt arrive at Ida's old house, Lecon comes out to greet them. He is visibly disappointed that Clara is not with them and also disappointed that his child is a girl.

The next two and a half years are monotonous for Ida. Her mother's health gets worse. Although Christine is not a pretty child, her fearlessness makes her special. Ida makes Christine call her "Aunt Ida," because this name allows Ida to distance herself from the child. Ida knows that one day Clara will come and that she might try to take Christine with her. Father Hurlburt makes regular visits to Ida's house during this time. Ida and Father Hurlburt play with

Christine, and while he helps Ida with her studies she helps him practice the Indian language. Ida enjoys Father Hurlburt's visits but does not want to let it show because she worries that he will stop coming if she lets on how much his presence means to her. One day, Father Hurlburt stops by to say that he won't be able to make the visit the next day. Ida says it does not matter to her, but Father Hurlburt says it matters to him. He says he can stay if Ida has time, so she invites him in for tea.

Clara finally shows up at Ida's house four years after her last visit. The two women hardly recognize each other. Clara has come to see Christine, so she goes into Christine's room and wakes her up. Ida stays in the kitchen and is so distracted by the idea that Clara is with Christine that she accidentally puts a hot ladle on her cheek, burning herself severely. When Clara describes herself as Christine's mother, Christine accepts it without question, not understanding the word "mother." Lecon, who is away working when Clara arrives, comes home drunk on Friday night. He has been in a fight and is behaving unreasonably, but straightens up when he hears that Clara has come back. Clara and Lecon avoid each other around the house. Lecon takes Ida and Christine to church, and then they all have dinner with Pauline's church family, the Crees. Ida can tell just from looking at Pauline that her sister is in love with Dale Cree.

Clara tells the story of her life in Denver with resentment. The nuns evicted Clara, and she then held and lost a string of jobs. Clara has stopped by the reservation as a break between her life in Denver and a new life she is planning in a new city. One night, Clara tells Ida that she has found a wealthy family who wants to adopt Christine, and that the family has paid Clara's way to the reservation to bring Christine back. Ida is reluctant at first, but tells Clara she will agree to the plan if Clara gives her until the following Wednesday to say goodbye to Christine. The next Monday, Father Hurlburt comes over. Ida suddenly tells Clara she cannot take Christine. Clara objects, claiming ownership of her daughter, but Father Hurlburt produces a paper that lists Ida as the child's legal mother. Clara is furious but powerless. She leaves that night. Ida sees Clara only twice more in her life.

ANALYSIS: CHAPTER 18

When Ida's relationship with Clara turns sour, it is Ida's first experience with betrayal. Clara, whom Ida believes is her close friend, turns out to have been looking out only for herself. Clara thrives on the attention the nuns give her and shows little or no concern for Ida. Ida's indignant attitude toward Clara now seems largely justified, but Dorris's technique of eventually revealing why each character behaves the way she does makes it hard to pass judgment on Clara. In the same way that Rayona's indignation toward Christine seems baseless once Christine has the chance to tell her story and Christine's indignation toward Ida seems misplaced now that Ida is giving her viewpoint, we cannot help but wonder whether Clara might also be vindicated if she were given an opportunity to tell her story. It is difficult to exonerate Clara completely, however, because after Ida tells her story Dorris leaves no room for Clara to explain her own motives.

In this chapter Dorris illuminates the origins of several details that appear in Rayona and Christine's narratives, and once they are explained we realize these details demonstrate Ida's genuine affection for Christine. One such detail is Ida's scar, a mysterious discolored mark on her face that Christine first notices the evening she expects the world to end. Ida does not notice the ladle burning her face because, as she is so deeply attached to Christine, any contact between Clara and Christine completely distracts her. Ida has previously tried to avoid or deny her affection for Christine by making Christine call her "Aunt Ida," as if putting some distance in their family relationship would bring about emotional distance. However, as we see in the narratives of Christine and Rayona, Ida's insistence on the title of "aunt" is only partly successful and even backfires. Ida's command that Christine call her "aunt" does not prevent Ida from feeling like a mother to Christine, but because the burn mark and other signs of Ida's love are difficult to interpret, Christine never understands that Ida genuinely loves her. Ironically, Ida openly shows signs of her love for her adopted daughter, but because these signs cannot be understood without knowing Ida's story, Christine never realizes that her presumed mother does care for her.

Ida's relationship with Father Hurlburt reveals that Ida is constantly plagued by the fear that the things and people she loves will be taken away from her. Her close connections to Christine and Father Hurlburt frighten her. The priest is the one person who truly treats Ida with respect, and because he is a party to Ida's family secret he has the ability to at least partly understand what Ida is going through. Even so, Ida has the irrational fear that Father Hurlburt will stop visiting her if she lets him know how much she enjoys his company, and she even tries to push him away so she will not mind losing him. Such fears prevent Ida from forging any strong relationships, especially during the two and half years before Clara returns from Colorado, and they cause her to turn inward and avoid depending on anyone other than herself. After trusting Clara and her parents only to see them betray her, Ida now fears to show affection toward anyone.

CHAPTER 19

SUMMARY: CHAPTER 19

Ida's mother dies. Lecon runs off a month later and Pauline marries Dale Cree. Ida leases her land and installs electricity and plumbing in her house. Around this time, Willard Pretty Dog returns from the war. Willard Pretty Dog was once the most attractive boy on the reservation, and was conceited and vain about his appearance. During the war, however, he stumbled on a land mine in Italy, and is now rumored to be hideously deformed. Willard has even gone so far as to paint the windows of his car so no one can see him as he makes his frequent trips to the hospital. Ida asks Father Hurlburt about Willard, and he says Ida should pay Willard a visit. Willard is so ashamed of his appearance that Father Hurlburt knows he will never see anyone at his house, but thinks he might be able to persuade Willard to stop by Ida's on the way back from the hospital.

Father Hurlburt says he will stop by with Willard the next Thursday. The night before, Ida turns on her radio and takes a relaxing bath. The day of Willard's visit, Ida has Pauline take her to the store, where she spends an excessive amount of money on groceries. Ida prepares dinner and puts Christine to bed. When Father Hurlburt arrives, Ida can hear him trying to coax Willard from the car. Ida goes outside and without even looking at Willard drags him inside her house. Once there, Willard settles down slightly. Father Hurlburt leaves and Ida tells Willard he looks better than she had expected him to. Willard disdainfully asks what Ida knows about anything, so Ida tells him her whole story. That night they go to bed together.

Willard begins to live with Ida. Pauline wonders what other people will think about Ida and Willard's relationship. Ida denies she is sleeping with Willard, even though she clearly is. Father Hurlburt does not condemn Ida when he makes his next weekly visit, and Willard joins in on their customary conversation. Three months later, Willard's mother stops by Ida's house and says that she has heard unconfirmed rumors about her son and Ida. Mrs. Pretty Dog acts as if Ida is Willard's nurse, although it is clear she understands that Ida and Willard are romantically involved.

Willard goes back to the hospital for more reconstructive surgery. While Willard is away, Father Hurlburt stops by Ida's house to tell her that Lecon is dead. Soon afterward, Ida realizes she is pregnant. Although she embraces the idea of being pregnant, she keeps it secret and plans to use the news to boost Willard's happiness if the operation goes well, or to console him if it does not. Ida rides with Father Hurlburt and Mrs. Pretty Dog to the hospital. When the doctor removes Willard's bandages, everyone is surprised to see that he is nearly as handsome as he was in high school. Mrs. Pretty Dog assumes that Willard will no longer need his "nurse," but Willard says he will be going back to Ida's anyway, and that it is time his mother understood that Ida is more than his nurse. Mrs. Pretty Dog argues that Willard can have any girl he wants now. Willard remains firm, saying that even though Ida may not be beautiful or smart, he wants to stay with her because she stood by him. When Ida hears Willard's words, however, she does not appreciate the less than flattering portrait he paints of her. By the time Willard is finished, Ida no longer wants him, and refuses the charity of his presence.

When people begin to imply that Willard must be the father of Ida's yet unborn child, Ida sarcastically implies how unlikely that would be. She never denies it outright, nor does she deny any other speculations as to the identity of her child's father. The only denial Ida makes comes when Pauline asks if Father Hurlburt is the child's father. Ida still associates with Willard, but she no longer feigns ignorance or stupidity. She wants to show Christine that it is all right to act strong in front of a man. When Ida tells Christine about the baby, Christine wants to know what its name will be. Pauline wants Ida to name the child after their parents, but Ida does not like that idea. However, when the baby—a boy—is born, Ida does name him Lecon, which she then abbreviates to Lee. From the day of his birth, everyone can tell that Lee is a beautiful child.

ANALYSIS: CHAPTER 19

Ida tells her story to Willard Pretty Dog but alters it. This alteration strips Ida's confession of the therapeutic effect Rayona feels when she confesses to Evelyn. In speaking with Evelyn, Rayona takes a step into real life for the first time in months. Afterward, Rayona no longer has the weight of a lie upon her, and thus feels relieved. Ida, however, tells her story to Willard because she wants to prove to him that she knows about suffering, and that his exaggerated self-pity is unmerited. In order to do so, Ida needs to show Willard that they have some common ground, so in her story she constructs an image of herself to please Willard. Though Ida's suffering has been real, she adds to her facade several attributes that are not true to her personality and pretends to be stupid and ignorant in an attempt to massage Willard's ego. Unlike Rayona's confession, therefore, Ida's talk with Willard actually takes her a step further into a life controlled by others.

It is only after Ida realizes she no longer wants Willard and is no longer concerned with pleasing him that she begins to act like her real self again. Ida's self-assertiveness is one of her lasting legacies to her family. After debasing herself to please Willard, Ida becomes determined to show Christine that it is acceptable to be smart when men are around. Both Christine and Rayona adapt Ida's advice and refuse to act stupid to please anyone. In fact, it is Christine's and Rayona's fiercely independent streaks that get them into trouble more often than anything else.

The people Ida is closest to react in varied ways to her affair with Willard, and their reactions are often the opposite of what we might expect. Pauline is judgmental and worries about what other people will think; it appears that some of Lecon's fixation on appearances has rubbed off on Pauline. Father Hurlburt, on the other hand, does not judge Ida when he learns that Willard has been living with her. Since both Pauline and Father Hurlburt are strongly connected to the church, we expect them to hold similar positions on Ida's life, but they actually hold almost contradictory opinions. Both see pros and cons in Ida's relationship with Willard, but Pauline is more concerned with the relationship's appearance of impropriety, whereas Father Hurlburt sees the positive effect of the relationship on Ida's well being. Father Hurlburt knows Ida and understands her, and he recognizes how badly she needs companionship. Although we expect Father Hurlburt to take a very moralizing stance, his sense of friendship allows him to set aside religious dogma and rules when he realizes Ida's relationship is doing her good.

Ida learns she is pregnant immediately after learning of Lecon's death, which can be read as a sign of the end of one era and the beginning of another. We have already seen this coincidence with Rayona's birth, which occurs the same day Christine learns that Lee has been killed in Vietnam. Indeed, throughout the novel we see this pattern of life following death. Lecon's death is a symbolic end to Ida's parents' generation and releases Ida from the confines of secrecy that her family has imposed on her. Likewise, Lee's birth represents the advent of a new generation and of a new set of responsibilities for Ida. With Lecon's death, Ida no longer has to take care of her family and their secrets, but in place she takes on the role of a real mother. The past proves resilient, however, and some traces of it remain even after Lecon is laid to rest. For example, even though she makes every effort to escape the past, Ida names her son Lecon. The name becomes "Lee," but the fact that Clara can persuade Ida, against her better judgment, to name her son after her father reveals the extent to which the past still has a hold on her.

CHAPTER 20

CHAPTER 20: SUMMARY

> *In my house, Christ was always being born or rising from the dead.*
>
> (See QUOTATIONS, p. 77)

Unlike Christine, Lee is a very fussy child. Christine is glad to be Lee's "little mother" and constantly takes care of him. Father Hurlburt becomes the head of the mission and becomes too busy to keep up his Thursday meetings with Ida. Instead, Ida begins to use Thursdays as time to spend with her children. The children naturally have questions about their identity, but Ida declines to give them any information. By this time, Willard Pretty Dog is married to one of the nurses who cared for him in the hospital. Every once in a while, Christine calls Ida "mother" to get on her nerves, but Ida never responds until Christine uses "Aunt Ida." Ida speaks Indian to her children, but they use English with each other and while they watch television. Ida has no preferences for one child over the other, and each of them requires a different kind of attention.

Christine becomes very immersed in her Catholic faith. Her favorite saints are the ones that suffered bloody martyrdoms. Although Ida is worried, Pauline believes that Christine's faith is unconscious reparation for the circumstances of her birth. Christine's devout nature is a contrast to her daring side, which comes out when she is around other children, especially Lee. When Lee tells Ida some of the brave things that Christine has done, Ida tries to make Lee promise not to try to copy her. Lee is not nearly so bold; in fact, he is rather timid.

One day Christine comes home a quiet and changed girl, and Lee brags to Ida that Christine was scared and that he saved her. After this incident, Lee finds new confidence while Christine looks at the world with new apprehension. Christine constantly expresses fear that she is going to hell. Worried, Ida consults Father Hurlburt, who suspects that Christine's anxiety may have something to do with a letter that people say the Virgin Mary herself gave to a young girl in Portugal. The letter is supposed to be opened at the turn of the New Year and is expected to tell one of two futures: either all of Russia will convert or the world will end. Father Hurlburt says the children in Christine's class are taking the message too literally.

Ida tries to talk to Christine about the letter, but Christine is set in her faith. Ida humors her, making a list of her sins and promising to stay home on New Year's Eve. Ida spends the alleged last day of the world with Christine. Lee says he is very skeptical about Christine's faith, and Ida does not try to explain to him why Christine feels the need for mystery. That afternoon, Christine spends a lot of time trying to make Ida look nice, and when she is finished, Ida is impressed. Ida gazes into Christine's mirror, astonished. The moment is ruined, however, by Lee's mocking laugh. As she admits that nothing is going to happen, Christine tells Lee, "You win."

At dinner, Lee, feeling his point has been made, tries to cheer up Christine. Lee decides he wants to stay up until midnight to prove Christine wrong. In response, Christine shuts herself up in her room and turns on the radio. Late that night, Father Hurlburt comes over to Ida's, and he and Ida go out onto the roof. Father Hurlburt asks if Christine had a bad night, and Ida tells him that she did. In the dark, Ida begins to braid her hair.

ANALYSIS: CHAPTER 20

Ida's comment, early in this chapter, that "[i]n my house, Christ was always being born or rising from the dead" continues the idea of death and resurrection from earlier in the novel. Ida means this idea literally, describing a religious calendar she has just brought home, but the phrase also reflects the fact that *A Yellow Raft in Blue Water* is partly a story about how Rayona resurrects the spirit and values that had been denied the women in the generations before hers. Ida is disillusioned at the age of fifteen when Clara and her father betray her, and Christine experiences disillusionment at the same age when the world does not end as she expects it to. Rayona is also fifteen years old during her portion of the novel, and often feels betrayed or abandoned, but she does not enter this cycle of despair. After two generations of disillusionment, Rayona is the first woman to truly find her place within her family. Thus, Rayona represents another type of rebirth—that of the woman in her family.

The strange and complicated genealogy of Ida's family reveals itself in the behavior of many members of her immediate family. Although Christine and Lee are raised as brother and sister, Christine acts like a member of an older generation, which, as Ida's half-sister and cousin, she technically is. This difference can be seen in the way they behave—whereas Lee is childish and requires much attention, the young Christine is poised and confident. Even when they are older, Christine is mature enough to exercise some control over Lee's life. Even though Christine and Lee live their lives under the incorrect assumption that they are brother and sister, they unconsciously act out the truth through their very different personalities and actions. Dorris places so much importance on personal background and family history that these elements affect the novel's characters even when the characters are not aware of their histories.

Most of this final chapter is concerned with Christine's loss of faith, which we have already seen through Christine's point of view earlier in the novel. Of all the scenes in the novel that are told from multiple points of view, this is the scene with the least amount of misunderstanding. For once, Christine and Ida seem to be operating on the same wavelength. When Christine tries to make Ida look nice for the apocalypse, both women are impressed by how beautiful Ida looks afterward. When Lee shatters this moment of connection with his mocking laugh, both Ida and Christine are angry with him. Interestingly, each woman is indignant on the part of the other, as Christine thinks Ida's feelings are hurt and Ida thinks Christine's feelings are hurt. This mutual concern is rare in the context of the numerous misunderstandings in the novel, and shows how close Christine and Ida are at this moment.

Dorris ends the novel with a return to the image of braiding to give us a final, lingering image of how his fractured narrative structure leads to a whole. Like a braid, the novel takes three different strands of narrative and weaves them together to create an over-arching story that is greater than the sum of the individual components. Each story contributes differently to the themes of the novel, but no single narrative operates independently of the others. Through the three different points of view, many aspects of the novel's events, characters, and characters' motivations are revealed that would remain hidden if the story were told from only one of these three perspectives. Thus, we have an opportunity to hear the whole story, something none of the characters in the novel has been able to do fully.

Important Quotations Explained

1. This scrap of paper in my hand makes me feel poor in a way like I just heard of rich. Jealous. What kind of a person would throw it away?

This passage is from Chapter 5, when Rayona finds the letter on the ground during her first day as a custodian at Bearpaw Lake. The picture of family life Rayona sees in the letter is an ideal one, with loving parents, a house with a lawn, and a pet. This vision is a far cry from Rayona's family life, which is anything but conventional or happy. Rayona feels like neither of her parents wants her, and the contrast between her life and the one in the letter is what makes that world so enticing to Rayona. In the passage above, however, Rayona does not feel joyful upon discovering the letter, and while it reveals to her that she is "poor" it does not do anything to counteract her circumstances and make her "rich." Therefore, even before we learn more about the letter, we can guess that it is doomed to fail as therapy, since it inspires envy without actually producing anything productive. Although she expresses some indignation that some children can be so lucky without appreciating it, Rayona does not realize the futility of envying the recipient of the letter when she first finds it, and the letter inspires more awe than anger. For a while, the letter becomes Rayona's exit from her life, from which she can draw the feelings of worth and security that she would ordinarily get from her family. Only later, when she comes to accept her real family, can Rayona throw the letter away and acknowledge that for her, it serves no more purpose than a piece of garbage.

2. [S]he lights Kent after Kent and the room fills with
    smoke while she kills the bottle. . . . Those nights I
    help her to bed.
       In school they had taught her all this crap about
    drinking and how bad it was for you. . . . Sometimes I
    found myself sneaking around my own apartment like
    some kid, hiding a bottle of V.O. in a shoebox and
    dreaming up excuses to satisfy her.

These two passages, from Chapter 2 and Chapter 14 respectively, demonstrate how Dorris shows us divergent points of view on touchy issues like Christine's substance abuse. In the first passage, told from Rayona's point of view, Christine is clearly a drunk, out of control and dangerous to herself. When she drinks, according to Rayona, Christine becomes so incapacitated that their roles are almost reversed, and it is Rayona who is forced to make the motherly gesture of putting Christine to bed. In the second passage, however, Christine speaks with righteous indignation, as if she were only a moderate drinker unjustly accused by a paranoid mother. Ironically, the language that Christine uses in chapter 14 unconsciously mirrors the situation Rayona describes, in which Rayona is the stern mother and Christine has to sneak around the apartment "like some damn kid." The difference between these two viewpoints is evidence of the power of subjectivity, and of how differently two people can see the same thing. The fact that they employ similar imagery, however, shows that even the most dissimilar viewpoints can be built around the same basic grains of truth.

QUOTATIONS

3. Rayona gave me something to be, made me like other women with children. I was nobody's regular daughter, nobody's sister, usually nobody's wife, but I was her mother full time.

Christine makes this statement in Chapter 13, and it demonstrates how the birth of Rayona marks the end of Christine's search for her identity. Christine's search has taken her through various stages and associations, but all of these have turned out to be unsatisfying, leaving too many questions unanswered. Before she says the words above, Christine lists all of her failed attempts to find herself by associating with others, attempts that we hear about as Christine tells her story. This passage emphasizes Rayona's importance to Christine, something we often lose sight of in Christine's dealings with her daughter. It demonstrates that Rayona is the central point of Christine's existence and that Christine's identity as a mother finally gives her a place to belong. Again, however, the quotation ends with Christine's highly subjective claim that "I was her mother full time." This description of their relationship is one that Rayona might dispute, especially in light of the fact that Christine leaves Rayona on her own when Rayona is just fifteen. For this reason, Christine's assertion that she is Rayona's "mother full time" is not enough to prevent conflict between the two. Before Rayona and Christine can be reconciled, it is necessary for Rayona to see herself as Christine's daughter full time as well.

QUOTATIONS

4.   I saw my greatest hits, the K-Tel Christine Taylor
      album, offered on a late show commercial: two or
      three bittersweet C&W cuts of Lee, a rhythm-and-
      blues section starring Elgin, a war dance song for
      Aunt Ida, and some rock and roll for my teenage
      adventures. Rayona was all ballads.

This quotation is part of Christine's musings at the beginning of
Chapter 14, as she reflects on life immediately after learning that she
has just six more months to live. The fact that Christine phrases her
retrospective in terms of music indicates the importance that Dorris
places on songs. Where many people might turn to visual images or
to religion to reflect on their past, Christine's first impulse when she
receives the news she is dying is to compile her life onto an album.
The styles of music she ascribes to each of the important people in
her life are representative of her feelings regarding these people as
individuals and their respective roles in her life, which shows that
music offers her the best way of expressing her complicated emotions. In the same way that Ida is most comfortable speaking in
Indian, Christine is most comfortable speaking in musical terms,
and in many ways music is a more adequate medium for her
thoughts than words are.

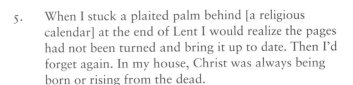

5. When I stuck a plaited palm behind [a religious
   calendar] at the end of Lent I would realize the pages
   had not been turned and bring it up to date. Then I'd
   forget again. In my house, Christ was always being
   born or rising from the dead.

Here, in a passage in Ida's narration in Chapter 20, we see how limited Ida's involvement with religion has been, and how death and
resurrection have a prominent role in the novel. Ida's words, particularly the phrase, "Then I'd forget again," emphasize how frequently the women in her family turn toward and then away from
the church. It is interesting that Ida mentions the "plaited" palm she
places behind the calendar at the end of Lent because the plait, a syn-
onym of "braid," is an image Dorris uses to represent the intertwin-
ing narratives of the novel itself. In the Christian faith, the palm is
associated with death and resurrection, and so the image of a plait
combined with the image of a palm frond could be read as a metaphor for the way the death and rebirth are always overlapping and
intersecting over the course of the three generations. Death and
rebirth in the novel appear both literally and as the the death and
rebirth of the characters' identities. The plaited palm is symbolic of
all the forms of death that Ida, Christine, and Rayona experience
over the course of their stories.

QUOTATIONS

KEY FACTS

FULL TITLE
A Yellow Raft in Blue Water

AUTHOR
Michael Dorris

TYPE OF WORK
Novel

GENRE
Coming-of-age story; tale of conflict among generations

LANGUAGE
English

TIME AND PLACE WRITTEN
1984, Minnesota

DATE OF FIRST PUBLICATION
1987

PUBLISHER
Warner Books

NARRATORS
Rayona, Christine, Ida

POINT OF VIEW
Each section of the novel is told from a different point of view. The first section is told from Rayona's perspective, the second from Christine's, and the third from Ida's.

TONE
The tone varies depending on the narrator. Rayona's voice is both jaded and naïve, Christine's voice is irresponsible and playful, and Ida's voice is resentful yet caring.

TENSE
Rayona speaks in the present tense, and Christine and Ida speak in the past tense.

SETTINGS (TIME)

The three stories overlap, but each story spans a rough time period: the 1980s for Rayona, the 1960s to the 1980s for Christine, and the 1940s to the 1960s for Ida.

SETTINGS (PLACE)

The novel opens in Seattle, and then moves to a reservation in Montana. Most of the events in *A Yellow Raft in Blue Water* take place in one of these two locales, although Ida also spends some time in Colorado.

PROTAGONISTS

Rayona, Christine, Ida

MAJOR CONFLICT

Rayona wants to belong and struggles to connect to her family; Christine wants to raise Rayona better than Ida raised her but struggles to convert her feelings to action; Ida wants to interact with the world only on her own terms.

RISING ACTION

Clara gives birth to Christine; Christine finds out that Lee is dead; Christine abandons Rayona at Ida's

CLIMAX

Rayona rides at the rodeo in Havre and finds the courage and confidence to confront her family's troubled history.

FALLING ACTION

Christine and Rayona are reconciled; Ida joins them at Dayton's house for their first cordial dinner in years

THEMES

Understanding different perspectives; the effect of past events on later generations; finding a true identity

MOTIFS

Pop culture; faith

SYMBOLS

Christine's videos; Ellen's letter; braids

FORESHADOWING

Foreshadowing plays a curious role in *A Yellow Raft in Blue Water*. Because the narrative travels backward in time, we see a foreshadowing of events we have already read about.

STUDY QUESTIONS &
ESSAY TOPICS

STUDY QUESTIONS

1. A Yellow Raft in Blue Water *consists of three distinct
    narratives. What effect does this structure have? Why
    does Dorris choose to present certain scenes in more
    than one narrative?*

It is important to observe that the three stories in *A Yellow Raft in
Blue Water* are all a part of a larger story. The tales of Rayona,
Christine, and Ida all intermingle as the novel progresses, and each
story supports and completes the others. This structure forces us to
take a more active part in our reading, and we play the part of detec-
tive, slowly gathering information about the characters and their
lives. What is crucial here is not just that one narrator describes
events that the others may not, but that the different narrators provide explanations for the strange behavior and events we see at earlier points in the novel. Each character's story seems like the whole
story as we read it, but the subjectivity of that particular character's
narrative becomes apparent when we read what the other narrators
have to say.

This effect is especially strong when different characters produce
their own descriptions of the same event or scene. We learn a lot
about the characters by examining what details they choose to focus
on and how they interpret them. At times, Ida, Christine, and Rayona make the same event seem like three different events, which
reveals that their stories are shaped more deeply by their personalities than by actual occurrences. Therefore, by telling the story
through three different narrators, Dorris allows us to come up with
our own opinion of the novel's events and characters and to avoid
being swayed by the words of only one narrator.

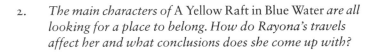

2.   *The main characters of* A Yellow Raft in Blue Water *are all
     looking for a place to belong. How do Rayona's travels
     affect her and what conclusions does she come up with?*

Each character assumes different identities over the course of the
novel, and their journeys allow them to discover which of these
identities, if any, will work out for them in the end. Rayona is a
particularly good example of how the characters discover themselves on their journeys. Rayona often laments the fact that she
does not fit in, has no natural place to call home, and is an outsider
everywhere she goes, mostly because of her dark skin and her
abnormal height and lankiness. She creates an imaginary identity
to help her better relate to others and to boost her self-esteem.
When reality intrudes on her imaginary world, however, Rayona
finally finds herself placed in the real world and earns the admiration of her peers with her bravery at the rodeo. Having gained
some respect, Rayona makes peace with Christine and is finally
able to establish a rapport with her that makes Rayona realize how
precious her family really is.

Before she comes to these conclusions, however, Rayona's
search for a place to belong leads her to try on all sorts of false
identities, and she tries to make herself as average as she can and
conform to the standards of whatever group she wants to join.
While at Bearpaw Lake State Park, Rayona tries to look like Ellen,
while on the reservation she wishes she looked like Annabelle.
Rayona also changes more than her physical appearance and joins
a religious group to fit in, even though she is not especially
impressed with Father Tom's ecclesiastical jargon. As these different identities disappoint her, however, Rayona comes closer to discovering who she really is. While Rayona's travels are filled with
pain and disappointment, they allow her to dispense with her fantasies about more traditional families and lifestyles and grow comfortable with her own family.

3.   *In the novel, the events of the past affect the lives of characters who are too young to know these events have occurred. In what ways do these family secrets affect the different characters of the novel? Are these effects lessened or amplified by the fact that they are kept secret?*

Most of the novel's secrets originate with Ida and her decision to pose as Christine's mother. Having to keep so many secrets is a burden for Ida and makes her turn inward and become reluctant to trust others, but the fact that she never acknowledges this turbulent period does not make its effects vanish. The secrets born in Ida's early life create many of the conditions that pervade the lives of future generations. For example, Ida initially makes Christine call her "Aunt Ida" because she knows Christine's real mother will eventually come home and she does not want Christine and herself to become too attached to each other. However, this title eventually becomes permanent and Christine takes it as a sign of Ida's embarrassment over her. Later, the title "Aunt Ida" is also imposed on Rayona and has the same alienating effect. Because Ida is so close-mouthed about the genealogy of her family, Christine is essentially fatherless, has no ancestors of whom she is aware, and consequently has trouble understanding their identities. To compensate, Christine has to try on a number of identities, which causes her a great deal of pain and disappointment. This identity crisis is likewise passed on to Rayona, who, like her mother, spends a lot of time drifting without really knowing where she fits in. In this sense, then, the hidden secrets of Ida's time continue to haunt her adopted daughter and granddaughter.

SUGGESTED ESSAY TOPICS

1. Dorris uses the images of water and rain frequently in his text. Discuss the significance of these images with relation to the themes and structure of the novel.

2. Religion plays a major role in the novel and appears in a variety of different ways. Discuss the various appearances of religion and its significance to the text. What is the difference between Father Hurlburt and Father Tom? Do characters have to be affiliated with the church to be religious?

3. Each narrator makes references to the popular culture of her time. What is the effect of such references within the novel? Be sure to consider elements of culture that are not necessarily linked to a specific era or point in time.

4. By presenting three different narratives in his novel, Dorris highlights the fact that all stories are inherently subjective. In what ways does this subjectivity come across in each of these narratives? Is the narrator conscious of it? Is there a definite right or wrong viewpoint in this novel?

5. How do Christine and Rayona use images of planes and flying in their narratives? What is the significance of these images? Do such images come up in Ida's story?

6. Discuss the role of escapism in *A Yellow Raft in Blue Water*. How does each character escape his or her reality? What is the result?

QUESTIONS & ESSAYS

Review & Resources

Quiz

1. Why does Christine go to the hospital so often?

   A. She has cancer
   B. She is a nurse
   C. She has a heart problem
   D. She drinks too much and has liver damage

2. Who is Elgin?

   A. A doctor
   B. Christine's husband and Rayona's father
   C. Christine's husband but not Rayona's father
   D. Rayona's father but not Christine's husband

3. Where does Christine want to go to kill herself?

   A. Point Defiance Park
   B. The quarry
   C. An amusement park
   D. A cliff

4. Why does Christine get a membership to Village Video?

   A. Because she just got a new VCR
   B. Because it only costs ninety-nine cents
   C. Because Rayona wants her to
   D. Because there is a specific video she wants there

5. What activity does Ida most enjoy around the house?

   A. Sewing
   B. Cleaning
   C. Listening to the radio
   D. Watching soap operas

6. What group does Rayona join on the reservation?

    A. The God Squad
    B. Teens for Christ
    C. The Committee for Christian Affairs
    D. The Mickey Mouse Club

7. Where does Rayona end up going with Father Tom?

    A. A state park
    B. Seattle
    C. A rodeo
    D. A parking lot

8. Where does Rayona meet Sky?

    A. On the reservation
    B. At Dayton's house
    C. In Seattle
    D. At the entrance to the state park

9. What job does Rayona get at Bearpaw Lake?

    A. Cook
    B. Trash collector
    C. Swim instructor
    D. Waitress

10. What does Rayona find on the ground at Bearpaw Lake?

    A. A letter
    B. A turtle
    C. A new shoe
    D. An old shoe

11. Where do Sky and Evelyn take Rayona?

    A. The circus
    B. Seattle
    C. A rodeo
    D. A foster home

REVIEW & RESOURCES

12. What happens to Christine on the night the world is supposed to end?

    A.   She comes home drunk
    B.   She loses her religious faith
    C.   She is hit by a car
    D.   Dayton dumps her

13. What obligation does Lee try to avoid that Christine urges him to follow?

    A.   Joining the tribal council
    B.   Serving in Vietnam
    C.   Participating in one of the local festivals
    D.   Participating in the rodeo

14. What do Christine and Elgin first talk about when they meet?

    A.   The fact that Lee is missing in action
    B.   Native American culture
    C.   Their parents
    D.   Their childhoods

15. What happens at Point Defiance Park?

    A.   Elgin and Christine break up
    B.   Ida talks with Willard Pretty Dog
    C.   Elgin gives Christine a ring
    D.   Rayona is conceived, and Elgin proposes to Christine

16. What surprise does Christine get when she returns to the reservation for Lee's funeral?

    A.   Ida tells her that Clara is her biological mother
    B.   Christine learns that many people blame her for Lee's death
    C.   Christine finds out Dayton is married
    D.   Christine finds out Dayton was convicted of child molestation

17. What news does Christine get at the IHS during her last visit before she takes Rayona to the reservation?

   A. She has to start a new, very expensive liver medication, or she will die within six months
   B. She does not need to come back to the IHS again because she isn't really that sick
   C. She has cancer
   D. She has worn out her liver and pancreas and has about six months to live

18. What does Rayona throw away when she and her mother go to pick up Babe?

   A. A bubblegum wrapper with a boy's phone number on it
   B. The letter she finds at Bearpaw Lake
   C. A bubblegum wrapper with Evelyn's phone number on it
   D. Christine's turtle ring

19. What is Ida's biological relationship to Christine?

   A. They are sisters
   B. They are half-sisters and cousins
   C. Ida is Christine's mother
   D. Ida is Christine's aunt

20. Why is Ida allowed to keep Christine even though Clara is Christine's real mother?

   A. Tribal law says that whoever cares for a child is that child's legal parent
   B. A legal document lists Ida as Christine's mother
   C. Father Hurlburt quotes the biblical story of King Solomon, which implies that someone who really cares about a child is that child's true mother
   D. Ida threatens to blackmail Clara

21. Who is Lee's father?

   A. Lecon, Ida's father
   B. Father Hurlburt
   C. Willard Pretty Dog
   D. Dayton

22. Who visits Ida's house on the night the world is supposed to end?

   A. Elgin
   B. Father Hurlburt
   C. Lecon
   D. Willard Pretty Dog

23. When Christine moves in with Dayton, what does she find out about him?

   A. That he is an alcoholic
   B. That he actually did serve in Vietnam
   C. That he was convicted of child molestation
   D. That he writes poetry

24. When do Rayona and Ellen finally meet?

   A. When Ellen comes to eat at Evelyn's diner
   B. At a party
   C. At the rodeo
   D. At a Teens for Christ Jamboree

25. Whose place does Rayona take in the rodeo?

   A. Father Tom's
   B. Sky's
   C. Annabelle's
   D. Foxy's

SUGGESTIONS FOR FURTHER READING

DORRIS, MICHAEL. *Paper Trail*. New York: Harper Collins, 1994.

———. *The Broken Cord*. New York: Harper & Row, 1989.

DORRIS, MICHAEL AND LOUISE ERDRICH. *Conversations with Louise Erdrich and Michael Dorris*. Eds. Allan Chavkin and Nancy Feyl Chavkin. Jackson: University Press of Mississippi, 1994.

ERDRICH, LOUISE AND MICHAEL DORRIS. *Route 2 (U.S. Highway 2: Description and Travel)*. Northridge, California: Lord John Press, 1990.

REVIEW & RESOURCES

SparkNotes Study Guides: